Posh Nosh

Author: Lannice Snyman
Wine notes: Dave Swingler
Design: Petaldesign
Photographer: Neil Corder
Stylist: Tamsin Snyman

Posh Nosh

fabulous food for family and friends

Lannice Snyman

Posh refers to something that's swanky and
luxurious: 'haute' in cuisine-speak.
Nosh, on the other hand, is slang for 'a meal or snack'
or 'to nibble or eat'. The words seem contradictory,
yet are entirely fitting for the title of this book,
conjuring up a meal that's special but not intimidating.
My kind of food!

Lannice Snyman

PUBLISHERS

ACKNOWLEDGEMENTS:

Chris Bradburn of **Clay Café** for the unique hand-crafted plates and bowls that augmented the family's stock of crockery used in the photographs.

Ivan Lawrence of **Mariner's Wharf** seafood emporium, for providing fresh, photogenic seafood for the photographs.

Johannes Laubser of **Fair Cape Dairies** for welcoming us onto his patch of paradise to photograph his cows, ostriches, chickens and children.

The family at **Joostenberg Deli, Bistro and Function Venue**, who let us loose in their butchery and deli, as well as on their historic farm, to photograph their produce and pigs. Special thanks to patriarch Philip Myburgh, and Christophe and Susan Dehosse.

Rooi Rose, for permission to use the photograph of Lannice on page 11, which was taken by Johan Wilke.

PUBLISHERS

First Published in 2005 by Lannice Snyman Pty Ltd.
PO Box 26344, Hout Bay 7872, South Africa
E-mail: lannice@lannicesnyman.com
Website: www.lannicesnyman.com

Author: Lannice Snyman
Wine Notes: Dave Swingler
Design: PETALDESIGN
Food Stylist: Tamsin Snyman
Photographer: Neil Corder
Digital Retoucher: Tim Lake
Photographic Assistants: David Leslie and Alastair Whitton
Copy Editor: Lynette Barling
Proofreader: Glynne Newlands

Pre-Press Production: Resolution Colour (Pty Ltd
Printed and Bound in Singapore by Tien Wah Press (Pte) Limited

ISBN 0-620-32302-7
EAN/BARCODE 9780620323024

For my mother, Lynette Barling, the poshest lady I know,
lover of the written word and, in her time, a charismatic actress,
consummate host, party animal and skilled journalist.
She has edited all my books with patience and love, working long hours
to find the flaws and polish the text so it's as good as it can be.
She is arguably the world's worst cook, but the very best guest.
I sometimes wonder which attribute is more important!

The Posh team

Dave – wine fundi

Posh Nosh was ages in production: months of lonely slog, exhausting hours in the kitchen, times of triumph (when a recipe worked) and despair (when it didn't), not to mention exhilarating tasting sessions when friends, family and fellow foodies clustered round the table for lengthy sampling sessions.

Things really come to life, though, when the creative team collaborates for the final sprint to the finish line. In a book as complex as this, they are the unsung heroes, rather like the wings an author needs to fly, or the frantically-paddling legs of a duck that seems serene above water, taking all the credit for being so clever.

In *Posh Nosh*, I had the finest bunch of professionals anyone could wish for. While each member of the team had a clearly defined role, creativity really knows no bounds, and the edges became distinctly (and delectably) blurred, with everyone working towards a common goal: to create the very best book possible.

Like most marriages, a partnership of wine and food is not always made in heaven. Which doesn't mean one should stop searching for an acceptable working relationship. To this end, I invited my favourite wine fundi, **Dave Swingler**, to work his usual magic in steering you towards the best possible pairing. A stickler for detail, he re-created all the recipes in the company of an independent bunch of tasters, and caused a considerable dent in his wine stock along the way. He also penned the chapter on The Posh Wine Cellar to get you started, and to round out your budding proficiency as a host of note.

Believing that the road to food and wine matching is littered with dirty pans and empty bottles, Dave brings a practical heartiness to the table. A wine enthusiast who earns his living outside the drinks trade, Dave is a longstanding writer for *John Platter South African Wines* and indulges his hobby corresponding for *Wine* and consulting to the hospitality trade.

Good design is pivotal to the success of any book, and it is a privilege to have worked, yet again, with the supremely talented **Petal Palmer**. She is tasked with creating the visual structure demanded by the text, making sense of it, and inspiring the reader to keep turning the pages. Her books have a distinctive stamp, keeping the reader interested by the element of surprise: pages that are sometimes restful, sometimes busy, always arresting.

But she does so much more, involving herself with the whole look of the book, including format and finishing touches, photography and styling, not to mention lifting flagging spirits, spurring the team on to greater heights, and encouraging us to do our best work. Everyone needs someone like Petal in their life!

Former senior designer in the Lifestyle division at Struik, Petal's work has been lauded both nationally and internationally, including several nominations for 'best in the world' at the Gourmand World Cookbook Awards, and a win in the Best Innovative Cookbook category in 2004 for *Modern South African Cuisine* by Garth Stroebel (Struik), which was photographed by Neil Corder.

Photographs in a cookbook are like precious rays of sunshine on a winter's day, and a cooling breeze in the heat of summer. They're also very often the reason why you buy a book in the first place. **Neil Corder**, finalist in the Mondi Awards, winner in both the Profoto Awards and Gourmand World Cookbook Awards, is a rare gem: a professional photographer who took care to learn the rules before having the confidence to break them and make each pic his very own.

In the middle of a frenzied schedule for the cream of South Africa's glossies, he worked tirelessly on this demanding project, skilfully crossing the fine line between photography, design and styling, bringing Petal's vision and my food to life, and helping Tamsin and I to see each picture more clearly, more creatively, more uniquely.

Neil – from the wrong side of the camera

Lannice – hunter-gatherer

Posh Herb – keeper of the herb patch

Courtenay & Michael – landscapers of note

Petal & Lannice – plotting the look of the book

Tamsin – style guru

Sensitivity, experience and intuition are the keys to being a good stylist, the link between the author and cook, and the photographer, requiring nerves of steel, an unerring eye for detail and the ability to oversee the whole project. More importantly, she needs an understanding of cooking, composition, food fashion and way more than a cursory knowledge of photography.

My daughter, **Tamsin Snyman**, is accomplished in all this and more. An inspired natural cook and exclusive caterer in her own right, she is blessed with the calmness required by this most exacting of tasks, and the patience to work with a sometimes extremely exacting mother!

No family member is safe from a food writer, and mine are no exception. Quite beside the obvious (they're taste-testers of note and an integral part of the publication from conception to birth), my husband, fishing buddie and soulmate, **Michael**, soothes shattered nerves, magics up single malts and cocktails on cue, and does the barbecuing for the photographs – not to mention designing and building our stunning kitchen and wine cellar.

Last, but never least, my other daughter, **Courtenay**, who shops, chops, encourages, clears away, tucks into left-overs, generally helping in a million different ways – and who has God's special gift of making everyone smile.

Let's not forget Posh Herb (keeper of the herb and veggie patch, plus a couple of secrets) and the faithful clean-up crew: gourmet hounds Maxine, Shadow Man, Daquirie Potamus, Storm Brown and Tsala, who stole our hearts (and some of the food) and sneaked their photographs into this book.

Thank you, guys. I couldn't have coped without you, and *Posh Nosh* would not have been the beautiful book it is.

Contents

Author's introduction

Get ready for sensory overload, to reunite with the real pleasures of the kitchen, where the joy lies equally in the journey to produce the meal as well as the guzzling thereof.

What inspires me most about food is that eating – a simple snack, a casual campfire repast, a banquet – means sharing. And coming together in this way is one of the most powerful and intimate forms of communication there is.

I'm pondering the demise of the twee little dinner party of calories gone by and shedding not a single salty tear at its passing. Not that I'm pole-axed with joy about what has taken its place: a barbecue ('Come around and bring something to put on the coals') or a restaurant down the road ('We're booked for 7.30; don't forget your credit card').

Not that I have anything against either barbecues or restaurants (a sizeable chunk of my life is spent at one or the other), but I feel short-changed in the emotional stakes.

Canapés with cocktails, a magnificently set table, several wine-matched courses plus Irish coffees afterwards may be pretentious (and unnecessarily complex) but I adore the fact that someone cares sufficiently about my company to seek it out and put together a memorable occasion.

Being strapped for both cash and time has brought about a whole new wave of home entertaining that makes Going the Whole Hog as dated as Beef Wellington and Stuffed Mushrooms. Which is a very good thing – the best meals are often the simplest.

Fancy dinner parties were few and far between in my childhood home. But mealtimes were always special occasions, richly blessed with family togetherness. There were often friends around the table. Conversation was light-hearted and unsullied by contentious issues (they were simply not allowed) and there was no television to distract us from matters at hand (eating and chatting) or to wrest us prematurely from our chocolate pudding.

We ate simple food, cooked by Joel Kambula, who was (fortuitously) on hand to see to our nourishment; our mom was (still is) entirely unenthusiastic about culinary matters and spent as little time as possible in the kitchen.

Most of the ingredients were grown or reared by my dad, an amateur but enthusiastic farmer. Free-range chickens, birds of noble birth and impeccable breeding (and eggs warm from the nest), were the order of the day. They died young, but not in vain.

Milk from our cows had a layer of cream floating on top. We dubbed it 'top-of-the-milk' and poured it generously over everything from porridge to bread and butter pudding. I helped my dad make butter from the cream, churning it patiently in a wooden butter churn in the cool pantry alongside the kitchen.

Fruit was home-grown and we often picked our own pudding, a favourite being ladies' fingers – small, sweet, thin-skinned bananas which we mashed and sprinkled with sugar (and sometimes top-of-the-milk as well for good measure).

On Sundays there were roasts: chicken; leg of lamb; joint of pork – with all the trimmings served in silver chafing dishes passed down through the family by a proudly beaming Joel.

On Mondays there'd be stew from the left-overs, but least said about these concoctions the better. When our parents were out, we joined Joel at the kitchen table and shared his delicious pap and gravy, eating with our fingers and marvelling at the fact that we were getting away with it. School lunches were peanut butter and bacon sandwiches – sometimes with sliced tomato as well – still treats I rustle up for family drives into the countryside.

When, years later, food would claim my heart, soul and future, childhood memories of fun-times around the family dinner table would be the benchmark of a meal's success. Text book perfection is all very well, but if the occasion isn't enjoyable, what's the point?

The rejection of mediocrity, stood me in excellent stead during my years as a restaurateur, and applies to recipes I create for books and magazines. It sustained me (enthusiasm miraculously intact) during 17 years as editor of South Africa's national restaurant guide for which I was required to go out on a limb and name my annual ten best restaurants. These represented kitchens

where chefs had grown, explored new boundaries, or polished existing skills.

Chefs who rest on their laurels and cling to past glories bore me witless; I prefer a meal that trips occasionally on its own enthusiasm, than one that plods pedantically through five courses of gourmet-perfect predictability. Growing is part of any quest for excellence. An exceptional meal knows little and cares less about stereotypical formulae.

Like many cooks, food journalists and culinary opinion-makers of the seventies, eighties and nineties, early years were stamped by a yearning to explore anything and everything – as long as it wasn't local! French cuisine, ruled. Then Mediterranean flavours, colours and textures knocked our taste buds into a tailspin (and some purists off their lofty perches). Tex-Mex, Californian, modern British, multi-directional Australian, and seductive oriental food fired up our palates, pens, and wooden spoons.

Yet on our doorstep our own culinary wealth waited patiently to be discovered. So I took time off to explore my own fascinating roots, journeying to every accessible (and some inaccessible) parts of the country, trips that bridged all local culinary divides and enriched and enthralled me. Some five years later, *Rainbow Cuisine* was launched, and changed the way traditional South African cuisine is perceived. The book has been reprinted several times, and has been translated for the international market.

My kitchen, therefore, is not traditionally South African, influenced as it has been by travels through Africa and to far-flung parts of the globe. But food is as much about heritage as it is about taste, so family roots and childhood tastes inevitably shine through.

My favourite recipes give preconceptions the short shrift they deserve. I adore the element of surprise in a dish, and there are many in this book. You'll find a seamless merging of down-home, real food with multi-faceted recipes that are no longer the primary domain of multi-starred chefs. There's a smattering of comfort food, retro-classics that everyone knows and loves, but with an edgy spin, cutting edge recipes, and international offerings tasted on overseas jaunts cunningly recreated for local palates.

This is the food I love – dishes where flavour results from the quickest of preparation time as well as those where the slow melding of ingredients results in subtle layers of flavours as they simmer or roast together: butter and pan juices caramelize unctuously; sauces glisten in every shade of brown.

Posh Nosh is designed for all pockets and preferences, and aimed at both novice cooks and more skilled cuisiniers. While set out in a classic way – beginning with starters and ending with sublime sweet things – there's no law that says you need go the predictable three-course hog.

If you feel like offering a bowl of soup with crusty bread, go for it. If the weather's hot and a salad will suffice, no problem. If you're in the mood to trot out a bunch of dishes and serve them buffet-style, there's no law against it.

Some recipes are multi-faceted, but they're essentially simple, hassle free and unfussy, leaving you free (as free as a cook can ever be!) to grace your own table and spend time chatting amiably with your guests.

Surviving your own dinner party with some sense of humour intact is top priority when formulating a plan of action. The trick is to avoid the stress caused by knowing that, say, in two Saturday's time your home will be inundated with a bunch of guests you invited in a moment of madness, and now wish you hadn't.

After years of practice, I've got it pretty much waxed: it takes a reasonably well-planned kitchen, bags of organisation, a fair amount of delegation and plenty of pre-preparation. This is where 'make-ahead' notes for each recipe will help; they spell out what's possible, what's probable, and what's not permitted under any circumstances.

Most importantly, you need recipes that work! A great deal of care has gone into making each recipe in this book perfect, and they've all been meticulously tested many times over. To please everyone, a mixture of weights and millilitres are indicated, with the equivalent in metric teaspoons, tablespoons and cups. With herbs, however, it's bunches and sprigs, and you're at liberty to use your discretion as to how much (or how little) to add.

There's really no need to treat recipes as gospel truths and to slavishly follow the instructions – let your own palate lead you as you make each dish your own. Flavouring is a personal thing, so please yourself. Chilli, ginger, garlic and coriander (my favourite herb) are good examples; if you love them, add more; if not, leave them out.

Timing, too, depends on so many factors: the size of your pan, the variables of your oven, the absorbency rate of flour, the size, weight and thickness of meat, fish or vegetables. A bit of common sense, in the end, should always prevail.

Fabulous food for family and friends is less about spending hours in the kitchen cooking up a gourmet repast. It's more about simply opening your door to your friends, uncorking a bottle of wine, and offering the meal you feel like cooking.

Posh Nosh is the result of a long journey of discovery; one that started in a Fish Hoek kitchen, and embraced the rest of the world before coming back home again to roost. It's about the joy of preparing food, a sumptuous celebration of 'cooking because you want to – not because you have to!'

The Posh kitchen

Just as hunger is a prerequisite to cooking a good meal,

love is the alchemy that makes it memorable,

and the lack of it has the power to trash your best efforts –

not to mention the most excellent ingredients.

More importantly, if your kitchen is a happy place, you'll be amply rewarded. If chaos abounds, it will show in your food.

Even the most carefree meal is a result of some degree of planning, and a reasonably well laid out kitchen and well-stocked pantry are non-negotiable factors. Size doesn't matter; being organized, showing respect for food, and selecting the very best ingredients does!

For those of us who love cooking, a pleasure shared is a pleasure multiplied. Meals are a natural extension of their preparation, so it's not surprising that the kitchen is the heart of the home. This is where the family grabs coffee and toast before heading off to work or school, gets together to talk, rustles up nourishment for body and soul, creates a feast for friends. More importantly, it's a sociable space, where children learn to cook from moms and dads, thereby passing skills on to the next generation.

I'm happy when I cook. It's my business as well as my pleasure; I cook because I have to and because I want to. So it's inevitable that much of my life is spent in kitchens: home, holiday cottage, makeshift campsite kitchens on fishing holidays and off-road trips into the bundu; my restaurant kitchen for a few fast-paced years; other chefs' kitchens when I'm gathering stories for magazines and books. Even friends throw open their kitchens at the drop of a hat in the hope that I'll cook up a storm for them while they sit back and watch.

The best kitchen spills into the rest of the house – leading seamlessly to the dining room and outdoor barbecue space and patio – opening it to all-comers, making it accessible to anyone who wishes to join in the action, and including the cooks in the conviviality of the occasion.

posh stock

Stock prepared from good ingredients simmered long and slow bubbles away happily on the stove while you get on with other things, and is easy to store: in the fridge for a couple of days; in the freezer for a couple of months.

If you choose to use commercial stock, find the one you like best, perhaps making it weaker so it won't overpower the dish. Add fresh ingredients to commercial stock: scraps of fish, chicken, lamb, beef or venison you're trimming up for a recipe, as well as a selection of vegetables and herbs.

Always taste home-made stock, and adjust if necessary. The concentration is important, too – thin with extra water if it's too strong, or reduce by boiling uncovered if it's too weak.

vegetable stock

- 8 carrots
- 2 onions
- 2 leeks
- 8 ribs celery with leaves
- 2 large, ripe tomatoes
- small bunch herbs (bay leaf, thyme, parsley)
- 2 litres (8 cups) cold water
- 250ml (1 cup) dry white wine
- sea salt and milled black pepper

Wash, trim and roughly chop the carrots, onions, leeks, celery, tomatoes and herbs, and place in a large saucepan with the water and wine. Cover, bring to the boil, then simmer very gently for about 2 hours. Drain through a sieve into a bowl, pressing on the solids to extract as much of the moisture as possible. Season with salt and pepper. Makes about 1,5 litres (6 cups)

chicken stock

- 1 onion or 4 leeks
- 1 rib celery with leaves
- 2 carrots
- 2 litres (8 cups) cold water
- 1 raw chicken carcass, with trimmings (not the liver)
- small bunch herbs (parsley, thyme, bay leaf)
- 12 black peppercorns
- sea salt

Wash, trim and roughly chop the onion or leeks, celery and carrots, and place in a large saucepan with the water, chicken carcass, herbs and peppercorns. Cover and bring to the boil, then simmer very gently for 2 to 3 hours. Drain through a sieve

into a clean saucepan, pressing on the solids to extract as much of the moisture as possible. Check the flavour; if you wish, concentrate the stock by boiling uncovered for a little longer. Season with sea salt. Makes about 1 litre (4 cups)

fish stock

- 3 litres (12 cups) cold water
- 1,5 kg rinsed white fish trimmings (discard bitter gills and entrails)
- 1 onion, quartered
- 2 carrots, roughly chopped
- 2 ribs celery with leaves, roughly chopped
- small bunch herbs (parsley, fennel, bay leaf)
- 2 strips lemon rind
- 24 black peppercorns
- sea salt

Combine the water, fish trimmings, onion, carrots, celery, herbs, lemon rind and peppercorns in a large saucepan. Cover and bring to the boil. Move the lid aside to partially cover the pan and simmer very, very gently for 30 minutes. Drain through a sieve into a bowl, pressing on the solids to extract as much of the moisture as possible. Season with salt. Makes about 2 litres (8 cups)

beef stock

- 1,5 kg veal or beef bones (or use lamb or venison bones, depending on the recipe)
- 2 onions, quartered
- 2 carrots, quartered
- 3 ribs celery with leaves, roughly chopped
- 80ml (⅓ cup) vegetable oil
- 100g tin tomato paste
- 250ml (1 cup) dry red wine
- 2 litres (8 cups) cold water
- small bunch herbs (parsley, thyme, bay leaf)
- sea salt and milled black pepper

Set the oven at 180°C. Place the bones in a large roaster with the onions, carrots and celery. Pour over the oil, then roast uncovered for about 2 hours until well browned. Turn the ingredients occasionally. Mix together the tomato paste and wine, and pour in. Transfer everything to a large saucepan. Add the water and herbs, cover and simmer for 3 to 4 hours (longer if possible). Skim the surface and boil uncovered until reduced by two-thirds. Drain through a sieve, pressing on the solids to extract as much of the moisture as possible. Season with salt and pepper. Makes about 750ml (3 cups)

The posh wine cellar

Few home cellars are planned, most evolve.

With the same care and enthusiasm that goes into creating the nosh,

a posh cellar can be a thing of balance and utility that sets it apart from the

vinous jumble with which many kitchenistas have to contend.

The dream of an underground vault, candlelight darting between the cobweb-lattice that links venerable bottles, is not a fact of modern urban life. Any space large enough to house the wine and allow access to individual bottles – that is cool and protected from temperature swings, humid but not a swamp, dark and far from vibration – will be fine. Don't, in other words, settle a case of your best on top of the washing machine next to the stove in front of your hi-fi speakers at the sunny northern window!

Wine remains very much 'alive' in the bottle. Chemical changes occur throughout its life until you pull the cork or twist the screw cap, as tannins, acid and wood components soften, fruit mellows and the colour of red heads for tawny.

Heat is the biggest threat. Sharp rises 'cook' the wine and cause premature ageing. Light likewise – the darker the better. If your accommodation doesn't extend to a basement cave, a central room without exterior walls is best as the temperature is more stable. Alternatively, choose a quiet space with a southerly exposure to minimize summer's worst. Wines are sealed not only to keep the contents in, but oxygen out. Corks need to stay wet from within (lying on its side) and out. Cellar humidity above 70% prevents corks drying and shrinking and the wine from oxidising.

When starting out and going shopping for wine, aim for breadth and balance. A wonder of wine is its diversity, which a good cellar will reflect. Nurture a clutch of bubblies should a romantic mood strike (or chocolate be served!), select whites for summer or seafood, buy in quantities of house-red to muse over while your hugely structured, rare (and expensive) feisty young nuggets mature, and don't forget the sweet whites and port...

Managing supplies is a matter of timing. A simple catalogue that records stock, rates of development and when each label is likely to peak is essential. The first challenge to cellar building is not buying enough (reds, especially) to start and drinking all you have too young. The second is treasuring bottles so preciously that they're too special to drink – and only doing so once they're over the hill. The trick is to check maturing wines periodically so that you have at least one bottle of a particular label left when it's at its best. That takes planning, regular tasting, a good memory, an even better inventory – and patience.

Remember to buy in as you drink out and, with time, you'll be enjoying reds a year or two older than the current release.

Investment or hobby? One pays, the other costs! Any wine bought for other than immediate drinking is an investment – in delayed, enhanced pleasure. Posh cellarists indulge in sensorial returns and leave the financial stuff to other counters.

POSH QUAFFING – a primer to food and wine matching
'White with white and red with red' is a conservative dictum that raises a wry smile for posh noshers. Fun, exploration and pushing the boundaries of taste and sensation require a little more leeway. But, while fashionistas will juxtapose old and new, retro with contemporary, over-exuberant food and wine matches can clash like cymbals.

'Contrast or complement' is a guiding principle. A fresh, tingling sauvignon blanc that cuts a rich cream sauce can lift the entire dish with contrast, while a waxy wooded semillon may be required to contend with – and complement – the powerful flavour of crayfish. Remember, too, that the headline status of fish or meat may not be the plate's dominant flavour – that could come from the sauce or side dish. Cook, taste and experiment.

Some culinary marriages are made in heaven – oysters and champagne, foie gras with sauternes, port and stilton – while other foods present challenges. Asparagus is a difficult customer, eggs by themselves make most wine taste metallic and chocolate continues to confound.

Wine no-nos include artichokes and vinaigrette. And powerful dishes may do better with beverages other than wine: extra-hot chilli, for example, calls for draughts of beer, the focussed flavour of a light-as-a-feather textured chocolate tart is better delineated by malt whisky.

The variations are myriad, but with a sole goal: both food and wine should be the better for one another. A sum so much more than its parts.

As for cooking with wine, always remember that if it's not good enough for your glass, it certainly ain't good enough for your pot!

There is always an air of anticipation when the kitchen
kicks into action, not least from the faithful hounds which
cluster at the back door in the hope of a few titbits coming
their way. They are seldom disappointed!
Serving a little something (snacks, salad, a full-on
plated number) before the main course means you're
serious about the meal — and your guests.
This part of the menu is (somewhat unimaginatively)
described as **starters** or, in more snooty circles,
hors d'oeuvres or appetizers. Call them what you will,
but be sure that they're subservient in the overall scheme
of things: they should tease the tastebuds —
never fill you up to capacity.

My favourite starters look sensational and taste even better – which pretty much describes the line-up in this chapter. A few make no bones about being snacks; some are salady compositions that lift our spirits without spoiling the rest of the meal; others are more complex creations that are sure to impress the pickiest of palates.

When deciding on the opening number consider the meal as a whole – balance is everything. In general, start light and move on to weightier and more profoundly flavoured dishes as the feast progresses, building up to a crescendo, rather like a symphony. Avoid repeating dominating flavours and headline-grabbing components such as cream, cheese, mushrooms, tomatoes and suchlike.

Never, ever compromise on the quality of your ingredients. If a recipe calls for something and what's on offer at your supermarket is less than perfect, adapt the recipe and substitute something else. Or change your menu. Simple as that!

If none of these recipes turn you on, take the line of least resistance and toss together a salad – a simple selection of fresh leaves, as is or tarted up any way your heart desires. If you love olives, add a generous fistful to the greenery. If goat's cheese is your thing, crumble it creatively on top. Capers are conversation-stoppers. Mushrooms are marvellous, either sliced raw or lightly steamed in a dab of butter. Other gorgeous garnishes include roasted seeds and nuts, slivered anchovies; croûtons or crostini – even poached eggs or sizzled oysters, when you're going the whole hog.

If you're feeling particularly frivolous, add flowers to your creation; as news spreads of their visual, flavour and nutritional charms, flowery salads are rapidly gaining favour. Anchusa, bergamot, pelargonium, borage, lavender, marigold, chive, rosemary, sage and nasturtiums are all common garden flowers that taste as good as they look. Rose petals – shredded or whole – are particularly toothsome.

A sublime dressing lifts the most mundane mix of salad leaves. Choose one from the following suggestions. There's plenty of room for experimentation; vary the oil (perhaps a dash of grapeseed, walnut, pistachio or sesame oil). Chop and change your vinegar: try raspberry for sweetness, balsamic for depth, sesame for an oriental flourish. Toss in with gay abandon your favourite herbs, roughly chopped or simply plucked from their stems with your fingers. If you're a heat freak, have no qualms about adding tongue-tingling zing with some chopped fresh red or green chilli.

posh salad dressings

honey vinaigrette

- 125ml (½ cup) olive oil
- 45ml (3 tablespoons) white wine vinegar
- 15ml (1 tablespoon) clear honey
- 2ml (½ teaspoon) dijon mustard
- sea salt and milled black pepper

Whisk the ingredients together in a jug until well combined. Makes 200ml (¾ cup)

soy, garlic and sesame dressing

- 1 garlic clove, peeled and crushed
- 80ml (⅓ cup) white or red wine vinegar
- 80ml (⅓ cup) olive oil
- 15ml (1 tablespoon) soy sauce
- 2ml (½ teaspoon) sesame oil
- 5ml (1 teaspoon) sugar
- sea salt and milled black pepper

Whisk the ingredients together in a jug and set aside for about an hour for the flavours to infuse. Makes 200ml (¾ cup)

cumin-scented dressing

- 125ml (½ cup) olive oil
- 30ml (2 tablespoons) red wine vinegar
- freshly squeezed juice of 1½ oranges
- 30ml (2 tablespoons) freshly squeezed lime or lemon juice
- 15ml (1 tablespoon) cumin seeds, lightly roasted in a dry frying pan
- sea salt and milled black pepper

Whisk the ingredients together in a jug until well combined. Makes 250ml (1 cup)

late harvest chilli vinaigrette

- 250ml (1 cup) late harvest wine
- 30ml (2 tablespoons) freshly squeezed lemon juice
- 60ml (4 tablespoons) olive oil
- ½ red chilli, seeded and finely chopped
- sea salt and milled black pepper

Pour the wine into a small saucepan and boil uncovered until reduced to approximately two tablespoonfuls. Remove from the heat and whisk in the lemon juice, olive oil and chilli. Season with salt and pepper. Makes about 340ml (1⅓ cups)

mustard seed dressing

- 125ml (½ cup) olive oil
- 80ml (⅓ cup) freshly squeezed lemon or lime juice
- 10ml (2 teaspoons) wholegrain mustard
- 10ml (2 teaspoons) clear honey
- sea salt and milled black pepper

Whisk the ingredients together in a jug until well combined. Makes 200ml (¾ cup)

thyme and walnut oil dressing

- 6 sprigs thyme
- 80ml (⅓ cup) walnut oil
- 30ml (2 tablespoons) white wine vinegar or verjuice
- 5ml (1 teaspoon) balsamic vinegar
- 2ml (½ teaspoon) dijon mustard
- sea salt and milled black pepper

Using your fingers, strip the thyme leaves from the sprigs into a small bowl. Whisk in the walnut oil, vinegars and mustard, and season with salt and pepper. Makes about 125ml (½ cup)

roasted
tomato tarts

Besides being delectable as a starter – perhaps with a small side salad of mixed leaves lightly glossed with balsamic vinegar and olive oil – these picture-perfect tarts make great finger food.

serves 6 (2 per person)

800g puff pastry
90ml (6 tablespoons) rocket and coriander pesto (half the recipe; page 68)
45ml (3 tablespoons) crème fraîche
100g small rosa, roma or cocktail tomatoes
olive oil
sea salt and milled black pepper
12 basil sprigs, for garnishing

Lightly oil the hollows of 12 muffin pans. Heat the oven to 200ºC.

Defrost the pastry if it's frozen, then unroll onto a worktop and cut out 12 rounds with a pastry cutter. They need to be a bit larger than the muffin pans. Lightly press the pastry into the pans to form roughly shaped tart cases. Bake for about 10 minutes until the pastry is crisp and golden.

While the pastry is baking, mix together the pesto and crème fraîche in a bowl. Roast the tomatoes in a little olive oil in a non-stick frying pan until they're hot and starting to burst. Don't let them get too mushy and wrinkled.

to serve Arrange the pastries on a large platter (a white one will show off their good looks best) and flatten the centres with your finger. Fill the hollows with a spoonful of pesto crème fraîche and a couple of roasted tomatoes. Season with salt and pepper and perch basil sprigs on top.

makeahead

These tarts are best when freshly made, so get the pastry ready for the oven, mix the pesto and crème fraîche, and have the tomatoes ready to roast. You'll only have to dart into the kitchen for a couple of minutes to put everything together.

poshtip

If you're not in the mood to whip up your own pesto, feel free to use store-bought stuff from a good deli instead.

poshquaffing

Medium-full with a hint of oak, a cool chardonnay-sauvignon blanc blend best tames the tomato and zippy rocket and coriander combo: chardonnay smoothes the edges while sauvignon gives lift. An option in the red genre is a light and fruity ruby cabernet.

crème fraîche is a wonderful substitute for cream, naturally thick and with a sourish tang. To make your own, sterilize a glass jar with boiling water, drain well, then pour in 250ml (1 cup) cream and 30ml (2 tablespoons) buttermilk. Close and set aside at room temperature for 14 to 24 hours depending on the air temperature and freshness of the cream. When it's lovely and thick, store in the fridge. As time goes by the flavour will become stronger and the consistency thicker. If you wish, dilute with more fresh cream to continue the culture.

Vine-ripened tomatoes are one of summer's greatest pleasures. They always remind
me of my grandmother's vegetable patch in the quaint mountain village
of Montagu. She grew tomatoes from the seeds of the previous year's crop, and
I loved helping her pick them and cook them up into jam.

with peanut sauce

Satays are my favourite Indonesian street-food bar none, and you find them everywhere, sizzling seductively over simple roadside braziers, tempting you to taste. Variations of the recipe pop up around the world, differing in components and fire. Here chicken is dusted with freshly mixed masala, and the traditional sauce ingredients are quickly whizzed together rather than being cooked.

serves 4

4 skinless, filleted chicken breasts
60ml (4 tablespoons) peanut or vegetable oil
roasted masala (see below)

peanut sauce
100g roasted and salted peanuts
6 spring onions, trimmed and roughly chopped
2 garlic cloves, peeled
1 red chilli, sliced and seeded
30ml (2 tablespoons) soy sauce
finely grated zest and juice of 1 lemon
5ml (1 teaspoon) brown sugar
2ml (½ teaspoon) ground cumin
125ml (½ cup) coconut cream
small bunch coriander, roughly chopped

Soak about 20 slim bamboo skewers in cold water for about an hour. Cut the chicken into slim slices and place in a dish. Pour the oil over and turn the meat to coat well. Spear onto skewers and dust with a little roasted masala.

peanut sauce Pulverize the peanuts, spring onion, garlic and chilli in a food processor to a fairly coarse paste. Whizz in the soy sauce, lemon zest and juice, brown sugar, cumin and coconut cream. Stir in the coriander, cover and chill until serving time.

to serve For the best flavour, barbecue the satays briefly over hot coals. Alternatively, sizzle under the oven grill with a strip of foil shielding the skewers to prevent them from scorching. Pile onto a plate with the peanut sauce served separately, for dipping.

roasted masala is one of my favourite flavourings. Dry roast 150g coriander seeds, 125g cumin seeds, 50g dried red chillies, 25g black peppercorns, 2 crumbled cinnamon sticks, 10ml (2 teaspoons) whole cloves and 15ml (1 tablespoon) crushed cardamom pods in a frying pan. Grind fairly finely in a pestle and mortar, then mix in 25g turmeric (borrie) and 25g ground ginger. Store in a bottle in the fridge for up to three months.

makeahead

Assemble and flavour the chicken satays a couple of hours before cooking. Keep covered and well chilled in the meanwhile. Peanut sauce is fine in the fridge for up to three days.

poshtip

Beef, pork, ostrich or venison fillet is equally delicious done this way, so use your favourite meat instead of chicken in this recipe, if you wish.

poshquaffing

Beer. Whether it's the fierce chilli, the partner-perfect peanuts or unctuous coconut matters not: street-food like this clicks fingers for a light, cool accompaniment. Iced, hoppy Pilsner styles refresh; heavier lagers and monastic brews – individual as they are – seem ponderous. Our enthusiastic taste-test panel made its way through all manner of wines before heading back to the bar.

There's a lot to be said for roaming the world by the seat of your taste buds sampling local delights. Everyone snacks constantly in Indonesia, and the variety and abundance of street-food is astounding. The air is punctuated by the aroma of smoke from wood fires, the waft of roasting coconut, the sizzle of satays and corn over roadside braziers, the fragrance of panpan leaves, and the nuttiness of roasted peanuts.

spinach, avocado and pawpaw
with cumin-scented dressing

Pawpaw always reminds me of sun-drenched days and magical moonlit nights spent on the island of Mauritius, a romantic place that smoothes the wrinkles in your soul. The cuisine follows – and fuses – French, Chinese, Indian and African influences, which inspires this salad. It's delish as is or presented with smoked chicken, fish or turkey.

serves 4 to 6

1 large bunch young spinach
cumin-scented dressing (page 21)
2 avocados
freshly squeezed lime or lemon juice
1 medium pawpaw
12 sun-dried pitted dates (optional)
1 red onion, very finely sliced

Wash the spinach well, trim the stems, then dry the leaves in a salad spinner and place in a bowl. Pour over the cumin-scented dressing and toss lightly to coat the leaves well.

Halve, skin and stone the avocados. Slice onto a plate and pour over a little lime or lemon juice to prevent discolouration. Skin, seed and dice the pawpaw. Cut the dates into slivers.

to serve The final assembly is pretty much a last minute business. Pile the dressed spinach onto a large platter. Top with avocado, pawpaw and dates, and garnish with sliced red onion.

makeahead

Salads are no trouble to put together an hour or two before serving, and this one is no exception. Cover with clingfilm and refrigerate in the meanwhile. Cumin-scented dressing, however, is best when left to mellow in the fridge for a day or two for the flavours to plump up nicely.

poshquaffing

Real riesling comes into its own with this heady salad. Its mineral tang freshens the luxurious viscosity of avo and pawpaw while highlighting the warmth of roasted cumin. And it's not overwhelmed, a brilliant support act. Chenin blanc would be playing it safe.

spinach was Popeye's second-best squeeze (Olive Oyle won by a whisker). It first popped up in Persia (now Iran) many thousands of years ago, hence its Chinese title, *poh ts'ai*, 'Persian vegetable'. Spinach later surfaced in Spain via North Africa, courtesy of the Arabs who were almost as fond of gardening as they were of roaming the world. By the late 1500s the English were munching it with huge enthusiasm, and today cooks everywhere prepare it in every possible way. Small, rounded, tender leaves of young spinach are better for salads than larger, tougher ones.

Happiness on a plate!
This dish is known to bring tears of joy to
the eyes of the most jaded gourmet.

sexy salad leaves,
goat's cheese and spiced nuts

Salads are stunning as stand-alone meals or as a precursor to a meaty main event. Here a marvellous mix of leaves is the base for the mouth-filling flavours of goat's cheese and sweet-spicy nuts, a recipe filched unashamedly from a special friend, Michael Olivier, who made it famous at Parks restaurant in Constantia.

serves 6

mixed salad leaves (rocket, butter lettuce, red lettuce)
200g goat's cheese, cut into rounds or slices
honey vinaigrette (page 21)

spiced nuts
200g unsalted nuts (macadamias, pecans, walnuts)
30ml (2 tablespoons) vegetable oil
125ml (½ cup) castor sugar
cayenne pepper

Soak the salad leaves in cold water, then dry well in a salad spinner.

spiced nuts Roast the nuts in a dry frying pan, tossing them about until they're evenly brown and the house smells like heaven. Sprinkle over the oil and castor sugar, then stir over medium heat until the sugar melts and caramelizes, and the nuts are crisp and golden. Lift onto a baking tray to cool, and season with a dash of cayenne pepper. Break into chunks.

to serve Pile the salad onto a large plate (or individual plates), garnish with goat's cheese and spiced nuts, and pour over a little of the vinaigrette. Offer the rest separately.

goat's cheese, also known as *chèvre* (French for goat), is available in a range of varieties and textures, and sometimes with coatings of herbs, peppercorns and wood ash. They range from mild and creamy to quite hard and strongly flavoured, depending on ripeness. In general, goat's cheese should taste nutty, sweet and slightly piquant. Chalky, soapy cheese has probably been over-refrigerated.

makeahead

All the elements of this salad may be prepared ahead. Honey vinaigrette is fine in the fridge for a week in a screw-topped jar. Spiced nuts may be stored in an airtight container for a week; lay on paper towel to absorb the moisture. Salad leaves that are washed and dried may be sealed in an airtight container or plastic bag, and refrigerated for a day or two.

poshtip

For a decidedly decadent variation, use fresh oysters instead of goat's cheese and spiced nuts. Shuck them, sear quickly in butter and flavour with salt, pepper and a squeeze of lemon or lime juice. Plonk them on top of the salad just before serving. Bliss!

poshquaffing

Sauvignon blanc is a classic match for goat's cheese. A sunny, ripe tropical style echoes off the cheese and fields the caramelized spice of the nuts. Bottle-fermented bubbly offers a racy alternative, mandatory if oysters are used. Sweeter tooths are accommodated by aromatic off-dry gewürztraminer, which fills in the edges of the piquancy.

Salad leaves are one of the joys of the fresh produce market, and we're spoilt rotten for choice. The trick is in creating excitement and equilibrium in equal measure by the inspired use of leaves and complementary goodies; texture and colour contrasting yet forming a canny cohesion.

sizzly grilled asparagus,
poached eggs and beurre blanc

Grilling adds a seductive smoky note to asparagus. For a super-sensual feast, round things off with perfectly poached eggs and velvety beurre blanc – a diet-defying sauce of butter whisked into an oniony vinegar reduction.

serves 4

500g green asparagus
olive oil
sea salt and milled black pepper
4 eggs
lemon or lime wedges, for squeezing

beurre blanc
30ml (2 tablespoons) white wine vinegar
30ml (2 tablespoons) water
15ml (1 tablespoon) finely chopped spring onion
125g soft butter, cut into small pieces
freshly squeezed lemon juice

Trim the cut ends of the asparagus spears and toss in a little olive oil. Heat a ridged grilling pan on the stovetop and grill the asparagus over high heat until well marked and tender. Brush the spears with more olive oil as they cook to keep them nice and moist. Remove from the pan, season lightly with salt and pepper, and keep warm.

beurre blanc While grilling the asparagus, combine the vinegar, water and spring onion in a small saucepan and boil uncovered until reduced by half.

Reduce the heat to medium, then whisk in the butter a few bits at a time to form an emulsion. Make sure the sauce doesn't become too hot as this increases the danger of it splitting. As soon as all the butter has been incorporated, remove from the heat and season with salt, pepper and a good squeeze of lemon juice.

As soon as the beurre blanc is ready, poach the eggs: bring plenty of water to the boil in a wide, shallow saucepan. Crack in the eggs, cover the pan with the lid, and turn the heat to low. It will take about 3 minutes for the eggs to be perfectly cooked. Lift from the water with a slotted spoon and drain well.

to serve Arrange the asparagus on four warm plates. Top with poached eggs and nap with beurre blanc. Serve with lemon or lime wedges for squeezing.

makeahead

Grilled asparagus and beurre blanc are best served warm, so prepare shortly before serving. Poached eggs, however, reheat beautifully. Keep moist in a bowl of cold water, then heat in a pan of simmering water for a couple of minutes. Another way is to fry them in sizzling butter (add some chopped herbs if you like). Baste with the butter as they heat through.

poshtip

Eggs for poaching must be really fresh – recently gathered from the coop if possible – otherwise the whites get wispy in the boiling water and they look a mess.
If you're uncertain as to their age, keep poached eggs in shape by adding a tablespoon of vinegar to every two cups of boiling water.

poshquaffing

The triple challenge of asparagus, poached eggs and reduced vinegar – wine foes all – calls for versatile vinous fare; don't blow your precious Alsatian riesling here. A fruity chenin blanc with a hint of sweetness provides a sensible backdrop to the main events.

Asparagus is finger food, which makes it great fun to serve if you think that the party needs something to break the ice. There's no better leveller than the sight of everyone licking their fingers!

scrunched smoked salmon
with caper and green peppercorn sauce

Remember when upscale restaurants everywhere draped smoked salmon over lettuce and garnished their creation with capers? This classic threesome is still enormously appealing, though here the capers form the base of a tongue-tingling sauce.

serves 6

caper and green peppercorn sauce
30ml (2 tablespoons) drained capers
15ml (1 tablespoon) drained green peppercorns
2 spring onions, trimmed and roughly chopped
125g crème fraîche
freshly squeezed lemon juice
sea salt and milled black pepper

salad leaves (cos or baby gems are best)
400g thinly sliced smoked salmon
drained capers, for garnishing
lemon or lime wedges, for squeezing

caper and green peppercorn sauce Using a mortar and pestle, pound together the capers, green peppercorns and spring onions. (This may also be done in a food processor, but it's much more fun to get up close and personal with the ingredients.) Mix in the crème fraîche, and season with a generous squeeze of lemon juice and a little salt and pepper. Transfer the sauce to a bowl, cover and chill in the fridge for an hour or two to thicken.

to serve Arrange the salad leaves on plates, and scrunch smoked salmon artfully alongside or on top. A couple of whole capers and milled pepper over everything – lettuce, salmon, plate, the works – helps the appearance as well as the taste. Garnish with lemon or lime wedges for squeezing, and a little of the caper and green peppercorn sauce. Serve the rest separately in case someone wants some more.

makeahead
The sauce is best made a couple of hours ahead, during which time it thickens nicely and the flavours merge. It may be refrigerated for up to three days. Individual platters of leaves, smoked salmon and sauce may be assembled an hour before serving; keep fresh in the fridge covered with clingfilm.

poshquaffing
The riot of luscious and zesty flavours deserves a sympathetic understudy, not a wine contest. Dry rosé (increasingly available, just ask) fits the bill with enough fresh berry fruit and body to hold its own. Looks good too. Caraway and dill infused aquavit or juniper-based gin offer bold alternatives, very well chilled.

capers are the flowers of the caper bush which become an oval berry full of tiny seeds. They're sold with tender stems attached in vinegar, brine or salt, and add a happy tang to dishes. Salted capers have a firmer texture and should be rinsed before use.

All the fun of this retro-classic is in the preparation;
assembly is a speedy, one-step thing.

avocado ritz
with a twist

During the *La Dolce Vita* years of the 1960s, every posh (and some not-so-posh) restaurant had avocado ritz on the menu. The twist in this version is not so much the ingredients (which make no bones about clinging to past glories) but the presentation which brings things right up to speed. Crayfish is the preferred shellfish, although langoustines, prawns and shrimps are good, too. And some parsimonious cooks I know add a few bits of monkfish or kingklip to the mix while no-one is watching.

serves 4

2–3 crayfish tails, depending on size
15ml (1 tablespoon) butter
60ml (4 tablespoons) medium dry sherry
sea salt and milled black pepper
1 ripe avocado
freshly squeezed lemon or lime juice
60g rocket leaves
parsley sprigs and lemon twists, for garnishing

seafood sauce
reduced pan juices from cooking the crayfish
125ml (½ cup) mayonnaise (page 102)
15ml (1 tablespoon) tomato sauce
pinch smoked Spanish paprika or cayenne pepper

Shell and devein the crayfish tails and rinse well with cold water. Cut into smallish chunks. Fry gently in the butter in a small saucepan until lightly sealed. Pour over the sherry, cover and simmer very gently for about 3 minutes until the crayfish is just barely cooked through. Remove from the pan and season with a little salt and pepper.

seafood sauce Boil the cooking liquid uncovered until reduced to a light glaze. Remove from the heat, mix in the mayonnaise and tomato sauce, and season with paprika or cayenne pepper, and a little salt and pepper. Mix in the crayfish chunks.

Cut the avocado in half, skin and stone it, and cut into chunks. Sprinkle generously with lemon or lime juice to prevent discolouration.

to serve Arrange the rocket, avocado and crayfish in martini glasses and garnish, sixties-style, with pert parsley sprigs and lemon twists.

makeahead

Avoid pre-preparing this dish at all costs, as crayfish loses succulence and flavour (not to mention all of its charm) if over-cooked or chilled after being cooked. At most, assemble no more than an hour before serving.

poshtips

To hot things up, add a touch of curry powder to the seafood sauce. For a spot of sweetness, use sweet melon (spanspek) or pawpaw instead of avocado. For the most eye-catching decoration ever, cook the fans of crayfish tail shells in boiling water and plonk them on top of your decadent creation.

poshquaffing

Rich shellfish and viscous avo, filled out by paprika, swamp less robust dry-white partners. Wooded semillon or chardonnay complement the flavour palette while heady port, gently cooled, is a successful foil for the more adventurous.

There's no reason why we shouldn't bliss out on this fabulous creation one moe time!

mushrooms on crostini
with crumbled pancetta

Some ingredients are destined for a happy marriage, like mushrooms tarted up with crisp pancetta. This is a great starter or snack; no meat required. Whole mushrooms look prettiest; slice if they're a bit too big. If you're not wild about crostini, spoon the mushrooms onto maize meal wedges (page 152).

serves 4

400g mixed wild mushrooms, small white button or portabellini mushrooms
125g pancetta
olive oil
freshly squeezed lemon juice
sea salt and milled black pepper
1 leek, trimmed and very finely sliced
1 red or yellow pepper, cored and very finely sliced
125ml (½ cup) cream
15ml (1 tablespoon) white wine vinegar
5ml (1 teaspoon) dijon mustard
4 slices ciabatta bread
rocket leaves, for garnishing

Rinse the mushrooms under running water while rubbing gently with your fingers. Slice or chop them, depending on size. Fry the pancetta in a dash of olive oil in a medium saucepan until crisp. Drain well on paper towel.

Stir the mushrooms into the hot pancetta fat (add a little more olive oil if necessary), then add a squeeze of lemon juice. Cover and steam over medium heat until lightly cooked (about 3 to 4 minutes, depending on size). Season with salt and pepper. Mix in the leek and red or yellow pepper, followed by the cream, vinegar and mustard. Boil uncovered until the sauce thickens sufficiently to coat the mushrooms.

to serve Toast the bread or grill on both sides under the oven grill. Better still, do this on a grid over the coals. Drizzle with a smidgen of olive oil, place on warm plates and spoon the mushrooms on top. Garnish with crumbled pancetta and rocket leaves.

makeahead
There's nothing worse than stale toast, so make crostini at the last minute. Pancetta may be fried and crumbled a couple of hours ahead; keep covered at room temperature. The mushroom part of things can be cooked the day before and kept in the fridge. Reheat just before serving.

poshtip
My favourite mushrooms are ceps (also known by their Italian name, porcini), chanterelles and morels. Cultivated mushrooms don't have the same depth of flavour, but are quite acceptable if you can't lay your hands on their wild cousins. At a pinch, use sliced black mushrooms; they make a more rustic dish.

posh**quaffing**
Pinot noir doesn't give a sideways glance in orchestrating the mingled forest-floor flavours here; a sensual hit. Mature cabernet/merlot blends also manage the earthy spectrum with rounded tones. If you insist on white, choose a wood-tinged chardonnay blend, but not so bold as to outdo the dish's inherent subtelty.

pancetta is Italian streaky pork belly, cured with salt and spices. It's way more trendy (and far more toothsome) than plain old streaky bacon, which you should use only as a last resort, when there's no pancetta anywhere in your orbit.

twice-baked two-cheese soufflés
with roasted red pepper sauce

serves 8

100g butter, plus extra for greasing the moulds
200ml (¾ cup) cake flour
500ml (2 cups) warm milk
100g gruyère cheese, grated
100g gorgonzola or blue cheese, crumbled
6 eggs, separated
10ml (2 teaspoons) dijon mustard
sea salt and milled black pepper

roasted red pepper sauce
3–4 plump red peppers, quartered and cored
50g butter
1 small onion, finely chopped
125ml (½ cup) vegetable stock or chicken stock (page 15)
1ml (¼ teaspoon) paprika

Butter eight soufflé dishes or teacups. Heat the oven to 160°C. To make the cheese sauce, melt the butter in a medium saucepan. Remove from the heat and whisk in the flour, then the milk, adding it gradually. Cook, stirring constantly, until very thick.

Mix the cheeses together. Set aside about half a cupful for the second baking of the soufflés, and stir the rest into the sauce. Mix in the egg yolks and mustard, and season with salt and pepper. Cool to room temperature. Beat the egg whites until stiff, then gently fold in. Fill the soufflé dishes almost to the brim. Bake in a bain-marie for about 20 minutes until firm to the touch. Cool the soufflés in the water.

roasted red pepper sauce Place the peppers skin-up on a baking tray lined with foil. Slide under the grill for about 8 minutes until the skins are charred and blistered. Pop the peppers into a plastic bag and set aside to sweat. Peel off the skins. Roughly chop the peppers.

Melt the butter in a small saucepan, add the onion and cook over medium heat until softened. Add the peppers and stock, and season with a dash of paprika, salt and pepper. Cover and simmer for about 10 minutes until the peppers are soft. Purée in a blender or food processor until smooth, check the seasoning and correct if necessary. Reheat shortly before serving.

to serve Heat the oven to 200°C. Butter a baking tray and turn the soufflés out onto it. Sprinkle with the reserved cheese and bake for about 10 minutes until beautifully puffed and brown. Place the soufflés on warm plates with hot roasted red pepper sauce spooned around.

makeahead

This is the ultimate make-ahead recipe for easy entertaining. Bake the soufflés the day before and no-one will be any the wiser. Cool in the bain-marie, then refrigerate. Turn out onto a baking tray and complete the second baking just before serving.

poshtips

This dish is the perfect choice to serve as a main course at a meat-free repast. Offer two per person with steamed or roasted vegetables, or a crisp green salad on the side.
A bain-marie (water bath) is used for gentle cooking in the oven; the soufflés are placed in a larger pan of hot water.

poshquaffing

Opulent, warm and inviting, the melty tang of cheese sparked by roasted peppers needs a brisk, near-spicy counter. One provided by a fresh chenin blanc in lighter style – not too fruity, sans oak, and very cold. On a chilly winter's night, ratafia (fortified chardonnay) would be an interesting choice; it has ample breadth and warmth of character to complement the plate.

Despite a tricksy-sounding title, this dish is simple to make and tastes magic. Even the most ham-handed cook can rustle up a white sauce, whack in some cheese and fold in beaten egg white.

In the bad old days of boring banquets and prissy

dinner parties, *soup* always preceded the main course.

But with the dumbing down of formality, entertaining

is more about what you feel like cooking rather than

that which tradition dictates. So soup is going main course.

Or not, depending your company, menu and mood.

In short, this versatile old stand-by is winning new friends.

My mother never pretended to be the world's best cook, but she loved entertaining and would invite friends around at the drop of a hat. Her favourite dinner party show-stopper was tomato soup, made rather artfully (for someone whose culinary repertoire was limited) with equal quantities of ripe and tinned tomatoes tizzied up with fistfuls of basil plucked from my dad's herb patch.

So far so predictable. It's the garnish that caused eyebrows to shoot heavenwards; a hard-boiled egg plonk in the middle of the bowl, white belly bobbing seductively in the depths of the broth. Her reasoning (obscure at the best of times) was the fun of watching her guests wrestling the thing with a soup spoon in the vain hope of finishing the dish with some modicum of dignity.

There's no need to make a huge fuss when making soup. But tasting it as you go along is obligatory. My favourites include whatever fresh ingredients are at hand, rather than studiously composed creations that require weighing, measuring and clarifying to get them just right. The biggest hits attest to the skill of the cook rather than the author of the recipe.

Soup can be thin or substantial, sweet or spicy, smooth or chunky, sophisticated or seductive. You can serve soup in any weather; while there's nothing quite like cosying up in front of the fire with a warming bowlful, soup is sensational served frosty cold on a hot summer's day.

Despite short-order cooks extolling the virtues of the 'joy' of stirring up a quick, instant cupful, making your own soup from scratch is something very special. Those who elevate home cooking to an art form will enjoy preparing their own stocks from patiently simmered bones, vegetables and herbs (check the recipes on page 15). But if spending time in the kitchen has more to do with expedience than pleasure, feel free to mix up an instant number from stock powder or a couple of cubes – you'll get away with your reputation intact.

Soup is easy to make ahead, reheat, and serve in a flash. And your guests don't have to be seated to sip it; simply fill small cups and bribe a small-fry household member (one who doesn't drop things too often) to pass them round. And you can get busy with something else. Like reheating the main course.

Serve your creation with a little something on the side; nibbly bits offered in, on or alongside the soup to round things out. Here are some great ideas in that department:

posh soup accompaniments

croûtons

- **sliced white bread** • **vegetable oil**

Pile the slices of bread on top of each other, cut off the crusts (toss them to one of the dogs), then slice the bread into cubes. Shallow fry in hot oil in a frying pan. Drain well on kitchen paper. Serve immediately, or store the croûtons in an airtight container for up to three days.

garlic toasts

- **sliced baguette or Italian bread** • **olive oil** • **peeled garlic cloves**

Set the oven at 180ºC. Cut the bread into fingers and brush on both sides with olive oil. Place on a baking tray and grill under a hot oven grill until crisp and golden. Flip the bread and crisp the other side as well. Rub the hot toasts with garlic and serve warm. Garlic toasts are also the perfect base for crostini. Simply add any topping of your choice and offer as snacky bits with pre-dinner drinks.

cheese toasts

- **6 slices baguette** • **125ml (½ cup) grated gruyère cheese**

Cut the bread into rounds and arrange on a baking tray. Top with grated cheese. Place under a hot oven grill until the cheese is bubbly and brown. Serve warm from the oven.

parmesan crunchies

- **250ml (1 cup) grated parmesan cheese**

Line a baking tray with foil and spray lightly with oil. Divide the cheese into six piles on the foil and flatten into rough rounds. Bake at 180ºC for 4 to 5 minutes until the cheese melts and turns pale golden. Remove from the oven, lift the cheese rounds off the foil and fold roughly like scrunched napkins.

grilled vegetable skewers

1 red or yellow pepper • **12 small tomatoes** • **olive oil** • **sea salt and milled black pepper**

Soak four slim bamboo skewers in cold water for about an hour. Cut the pepper into chunks and thread onto the skewers with the tomatoes. Arrange on a baking tray, drizzle with olive oil and season with salt and pepper. Grill under a hot oven grill for 4 to 5 minutes; they're best served slightly crunchy and warm.

cool cucumber and leek soup
with gingered cucumber ribbons

Gentle flavours rule this soup, which is equally delicious hot or cold. It's also fab in shot glasses with pre-dinner drinks. And gingered cucumber ribbons are delicious sidekicks to grilled or barbecued fish.

serves 6

1 English cucumber, roughly chopped (skin on)
2 leeks, trimmed and sliced
1 litre (4 cups) vegetable stock or chicken stock (page 15)
30ml (2 tablespoons) chopped fennel
sea salt and milled black pepper

gingered cucumber ribbons
½ English cucumber (skin on)
5ml (1 teaspoon) sesame oil
5ml (1 teaspoon) scraped and finely chopped fresh ginger
1 green or red chilli, seeded and finely shredded
5ml (1 teaspoon) cracked black pepper
30ml (2 tablespoons) white wine vinegar
15ml (1 tablespoon) brown sugar

Combine the cucumber, leeks and stock in a medium saucepan. Cover and simmer for about 30 minutes until the vegetables are tender. Whizz the soup smoothly in a blender or food processor with the fennel, and season with salt and pepper. Allow to cool, then chill in the fridge.

gingered cucumber ribbons Slice the cucumber lengthwise into thin strips, using a potato peeler and working down to the pips. Discard the core. Place the strips in a serving bowl.

Heat the sesame oil in a small frying pan, add the ginger, chilli and pepper and stir-fry for about 20 seconds. Add the vinegar and sugar and stir until it dissolves. Allow the dressing to cool, then pour over the cucumber and toss everything together.

to serve Ladle the soup into bowls or shot glasses and garnish with gingered cucumber ribbons. Or, if you prefer, offer them on the side.

makeahead
The soup may be refrigerated for up to two days. Gingered cucumber ribbons, on the other hand, look prettiest when they're no more than a couple of hours old, so resist the urge to prepare them too far ahead.

posh**quaffing**
Soup is fractious with wine at the best of times. Traditional sherry is adequate but oh-so-dull with this refreshing veggie duo. Kir Royale – bubbly poured over crème de cassis, the blackcurrant liqueur of Dijon – sparkles in combination here, lively and delicately fruity. Carbonated sparkling wine is fine, and substitute any red berry elixir if you can't find Burgundy's best.

fresh ginger is a heavenly flavouring, one that I fling into a wide variety of dishes without hesitation. Slightly spicy, vaguely sweet and peppery, the bumpy root of the ginger plant originated in South East Asia, where it has been used both in cooking and for medicinal purposes since the year dot. Choose fresh ginger that's plump and shiny, and scrape off the skin before pounding, slicing, grating, slivering ot chopping as required in the recipe. And remember, the younger the root, the more delicate the flavour.

a different
beetroot soup

Perhaps it's the colour – maybe the shape. But beetroot isn't a vegetable that inspires us to bound into the kitchen in a flurry of enthusiasm, bunch in hand, to try it in new ways. Most people I know (Polish and Russian friends excluded, for obvious reasons) even turn up their noses at that most distinguished of soups – bortsch. Here's a light and luscious variation of that classic soup, which is delicious hot or chilled.

serves 4 to 6

1,5 litres (6 cups) vegetable stock or chicken stock (page 15)
800g (2 bunches) beetroot, peeled and cut into matchsticks
2 carrots, peeled and cut into matchsticks
2 ribs celery, very finely sliced (don't use the leaves)
1 small red onion, very finely sliced
1 bunch herbs (fennel, parsley, marjoram)
2 whole cloves
sea salt and milled black pepper
125g crème fraîche, to serve

Combine the stock, beetroot, carrot, celery, onion, herbs and cloves in a large saucepan. Season with a little salt and pepper, cover and simmer for about 10 minutes until the vegetables are tender. Discard the herbs.

Lift half the vegetables from the pan with a slotted spoon and set aside. Purée the rest in a blender or food processor with the broth. Pour back into the pan and add the reserved vegetables. If serving the soup hot, simmer it for a minute or two to heat through. If you prefer it cool, pour into a bowl, cover and refrigerate.

to serve Ladle the soup into bowls, and top each serving with a dollop of crème fraîche to stir in while you're tucking in.

makeahead
Bung the covered bowl of soup into the fridge for up to three days.

poshtips
Young beetroot leaves, trimmed and very finely shredded, may be added to the soup when it's being reheated. And ready-cooked beetroot works perfectly if you can't be bothered with starting from scratch.

poshquaffing
Both colour and fleshy flavours call for a complementary tipple. Lighter nouveau-styled wines, gamay noir especially, spar with the individual beetroot character, while medium-bodied barbera offers succour when the former are out of (post-harvest) season. And then there's always a shot of vodka, near-freezing, in an iced glass.

onions come in an array of colours, shapes and sizes, and have different culinary uses, despite the fact that they're related. There are yellow onions (all-rounders with brown skins), milder, sweeter Spanish and purple onions (better for salads) and tiny pickling onions (great for cooking whole). Other family members include gently-flavoured leeks (preferred for stocks and soups) and smaller greenies – spring onions, shallots and chives (perfect for sauces and raw in salads).

Food, like eroticism, starts with the eyes, so take special care when
choosing your crockery and presenting your creation.
Which isn't to say you need to garnish with fistfuls of garden greenery!

carrot and turnip soup
like granny made

Let's face it, root vegetables aren't the sexiest of ingredients, but you'll become addicted to this hearty potage that calls for carrots and turnips, and an intriguing trio of spices (coriander, cumin and nutmeg). Parmesan crunchies on the side raises the game even more.

serves 6

700g carrots, peeled and sliced
2 small turnips, peeled and chopped
3–4 leeks, trimmed and sliced
1,5 litres (6 cups) vegetable stock (page 15)
2ml (½ teaspoon) ground coriander
2ml (½ teaspoon) ground cumin
1ml (¼ teaspoon) grated nutmeg
sugar, sea salt, milled black pepper
125ml (½ cup) cream
parmesan crunchies, to serve (page 43)

Toss the carrots, turnips and leeks into a large saucepan with a cupful of the stock. Cover and simmer over gentle heat for about 10 minutes. Add the coriander, cumin and nutmeg, and season with a little sugar, salt and pepper. Pour in the remaining stock, cover and simmer for about 45 minutes until the vegetables are soft.

Purée the soup smoothly in a food processor or blender, then pour back into the pan. Add the cream and reheat. Check the flavour and consistency, and adjust if necessary.

to serve Serve the soup piping hot with parmesan crunchies on the side. If you're not up to making these crunchy delights, store-bought croûtons are an acceptible alternative.

makeahead

You're welcome to make this soup a day or two ahead and reheat it just before serving. Parmesan crunchies are the least troublesome garnish, retaining their crunch for hours. Cool, then store in an airtight container.

poshquaffing

Granny would start with conventional wisdom and sherry. The adventurous may opt for fleshy chenin blanc with pulpy fruit, touches of oak and a gentle hint of sweetness: muscle to cope without competing. Granny wins. The breadth of food flavour demands a gentle medium dry sherry as bone dry bottlings elbow the soup off the palette.

carrots, beloved by bunnies (and other interesting creatures), are delicious and nutritious. Prior to landing on the dinner table, carrots were a fashion statement – their feathery tops festooned the hats and sleeves of high-society ladies of the Stuart court. They were initially classed as weeds and used as cattle feed, whereafter their image improved a tad – post-First World War nannies urged their young charges to gobble them up in the quest for curling hair – and in the hope that they would see in the dark.

parsley soup
with a touch of thyme

Parsley and thyme team up in this quick-to-make soup that sees herbs in a starring role rather than mere window dressing. The flavour of parsley stalks is important in the scheme of things, so don't discard them. And to capture the bright colour and fresh flavour of the herbs, cook the soup for a very short time. Crunchy, deep-fried parsley is an optional garnish.

serves 6

50g butter
2 leeks, trimmed and finely sliced
leaves stripped from 3–4 long sprigs thyme
60ml (4 tablespoons) cake flour
1,25 litres (5 cups) vegetable stock or chicken stock (page 15)
250ml (1 cup) finely chopped flat-leaf parsley (stalks and leaves)
sea salt and milled black pepper
cheese toasts, to serve (page 43)

crunchy parsley
1 bunch flat-leaf parsley
vegetable oil

Melt the butter in a medium saucepan and stir in the leeks and thyme. Cover and sweat over low heat for a minute or two until nicely softened.

Remove from the heat and stir in the flour, then add the stock. Bring to the boil, add the parsley and simmer for 2 to 3 minutes. Season with salt and pepper.

crunchy parsley Rinse the bunch of parsley, shake energetically, then pat completely dry with paper towels. Discard the thickest stems. Deep-fry the leaves in medium-hot oil until crisp. Lift from the oil with a slotted spoon and drain well on a wad of paper towel.

to serve Ladle the hot soup into bowls. Float cheese toasts on top and garnish with bags of crunchy parsley.

makeahead
The colour and flavour of parsley is best if the soup is served on the day it's made, so avoid preparing it too far ahead.

poshtip
For a richer soup (and if you're not counting kilojoules), replace some of the stock with cream.

poshquaffing
This ubiquitous herb is concentrated into a grassy rapier, and needs a liquid foil to match. Unimaginitive dry-whites get clobbered by the soup's flavour, but méthode cap classique possesses the body – and zip – to up the ante. Herbaceous, linear sauvignon blanc is an option for those not of champagne tastes.

parsley, a happy herb, is used in just about every recipe under the sun, quite besides its usual role as a granny garnish plonked on top of a completed dish. You'll find two types on offer: common moss-curled parsley, and more modish flat-leaf Italian parsley, which has the edge in the flavour stakes.

No herb patch is complete without rows of parsley, which has a tendency to attract snails in their droves. If you're averse to wild-life in your food, wash parsley well before use!

gorgonzola vichyssoise
with garlic toasts

Eyes light up whenever potato and leek soup is trotted out. This natty version
includes the surprise ingredient of gorgonzola cheese, which is blended into the soup
as well as crumbled on top. Serve hot or – in the traditional way – well chilled.

serves 8

100g gorgonzola or blue cheese
50g butter
3–4 leeks, trimmed and finely sliced (white parts only)
750g (about 6) potatoes, peeled and cubed
2 large sprigs fennel
1,25 litres (5 cups) chicken stock (page 15)
sea salt and milled black pepper
garlic toasts, to serve (page 43)

Crumble the cheese. Melt the butter in a large saucepan. Stir in the leeks, cover and sweat very
gently over medium heat for about 5 minutes. Don't allow them to gain colour, as this will spoil
the appearance of the soup.

Add the potato, fennel and stock, and season with salt and pepper. Cover and simmer gently
for about 20 minutes until the potato is soft. Discard the fennel, add half the cheese (reserve
the rest for garnishing) and purée the soup smoothly in a food processor or blender. Depending
on how you plan to serve it, chill the soup, or pour it back into the pan and reheat.

to serve Ladle the soup into bowls and garnish with the reserved crumbled cheese. If the soup
is hot, it will melt delectably as you eat it. Pass round a plate of garlic toasts.

makeahead

The soup is quite happy if made
a day or two ahead and kept chilled.
Reheat if you wish, and garnish with
crumbled cheese just before serving.

poshtip

A glug of cream stirred in at the end
adds luxurious smoothness and
richness to this soup.

poshquaffing

Classic vichyssoise, cool and
restorative, is best with dry sauvignon
blanc-based blends that highlight the
vegetables. Gorgonzola adds a twist
here that needs sturdier stuff. Chilled
white jerepigo offers sweetness and
a spine of alcohol: both engage the
cheese with aplomb.

potatoes are welcoming and honest. They can be anything you want them to be, from haute to homespun
(and everything in between!). Even when playing a supporting role in a recipe, they make their presence felt.
There are endless varieties, many of which are good for soup. Avoid waxy types, which become glutinous as they
cook, and no good for mashing or puréeing.

crayfish cappuccino
glazed with borrie foam

Most of us are addicted to anything edible that has spent its life underwater, be it swimming, crawling, burrowing in the sand or clinging to wave-washed rocks. But nothing is more luxurious than crayfish. Chunks of it loll about in this velvety soup that is snazzily capped with glazed borrie foam. If there's no crayfish about, scallops and peeled prawns are equally delicious in this recipe.

serves 4

1 litre (4 cups) fish stock (page 15)
250g (2–3) crayfish tails, in the shell
100g butter
30ml (2 tablespoons) chopped fennel
30ml (2 tablespoons) snipped chives
125ml (½ cup) dry white wine
125ml (½ cup) cream
90ml (6 tablespoons) cake flour
sea salt and milled black pepper

borrie foam
250ml (1 cup) cream
1ml (¼ teaspoon) turmeric (borrie)

Warm the stock in a small saucepan. Shell and devein the crayfish, and rinse everything clean – meat, shells, the lot. Cut the meat into smallish chunks. Add the shells to the stock, cover and simmer gently for about 10 minutes to extract all the flavour from the shells.

Heat half the butter in a medium saucepan and lightly fry the crayfish chunks; you just want to seal them without cooking them through. Lift from the pan with a slotted spoon and set aside. Add the fennel, chives and wine to the pan, and boil uncovered until the liquid has reduced by half. Add the cream and reduce again by half to intensify the flavour.

Melt the remaining butter in a large saucepan. Remove from the heat and blend in the flour. Strain in the hot stock, stirring constantly, then cover and simmer over medium heat for about 5 minutes. Season with salt and pepper. Add the wine and cream reduction with the crayfish chunks and heat through.

to serve Heat the oven grill. Lightly whip the topping cream until it forms soft peaks, then gently mix in the turmeric. Ladle the soup into hot cups or soup bowls, float borrie foam on top and glaze under the grill.

makeahead
It's preferable not to, but if you must, prepare the soup prior to the point of adding the crayfish, then cover and chill for a day. Reheat the soup, add the crayfish and glaze with borrie foam just before serving.

poshtip
Fish stock is the flavour base of this soup, so prepare it with bags of love. If you really can't be bothered to make fish stock, use light chicken stock. The crayfish shells will add their magical flavour and no-one will be any the wiser.

poshquaffing
Unctuous waves of shellfish flavour, with borrie to boot, wash away most wines. A thrilling counter to all this opulence is the minerally tang of fine dry riesling – it cuts and parries with a tingle. Serious gewürztraminer (dry, even oaked, rare but available) has muscle for those seeking bolder wares. Avoid wooded chardonnay; it's just too much.

Crayfish have many names, but they're edible bliss in any language. In polite company they answer to kreef and rock lobster, their official title. Divers call them 'crawlies' and wouldn't dream of using them in soup, preferring their catch simply boiled in a tin over a fire on the beach within minutes of being hauled from the deep.

indonesian-style
seafood soup

This creation, inspired by a sojourn on the island of Bali, is crammed with typical Indonesian flavourings of garlic, ginger, chilli, lemon grass and coriander. Your preference may well be for a little more or less spice, so feel free to adjust the quantities. Fish stock is pivotal to success, so do make your own. Alternatively, substitute light chicken or vegetable stock (page 15). Nuggets of crayfish may be used instead of prawns, if you wish.

serves 8

800g filleted fish
16 black mussels, scrubbed clean and bearded
16 large prawns
1 onion, sliced
vegetable oil
2 litres (8 cups) fish stock (page 15)
500ml (2 cups) coconut cream
2 lemon leaves, lightly bruised
10cm stem lemon grass, outer layer removed, lightly bruised
6 slices fresh ginger
4 garlic cloves, peeled and finely chopped
2ml (½ teaspoon) turmeric (borrie)
5ml (1 teaspoon) brown sugar
30ml (2 tablespoons) fish sauce
30ml (2 tablespoons) rice wine or medium dry sherry
1 red or green chilli, seeded and finely sliced
small bunch coriander, chopped (leaves and stems)
sea salt and milled black pepper

Skin the fish and cut it into large chunks. Rinse the mussels in cold water, then tip into a colander to drain. Peel the prawns.

Fry the onion in a little oil in a large saucepan until golden. Stir in the stock and coconut cream, then the lemon leaves, lemon grass, ginger and garlic. Simmer very gently for about 15 minutes, partially covered. Set aside for 15 minutes for the flavours to infuse.

Shortly before serving, add the fish and prawns to the soup with the turmeric, brown sugar, fish sauce, rice wine or sherry, chilli and half the chopped coriander. Flavour with a little salt and pepper. Simmer uncovered for about 3 minutes until the seafood is barely cooked.

Add the mussels, cover and simmer just until the shells open, which is when they're cooked. Discard any that remain closed.

to serve Serve the soup hot in wide-brimmed bowls garnished with the remaining coriander.

makeahead

There's a natural half-way stage in this recipe: after the soup has been cooked and before the seafood is added. Chill seafood and soup separately for up to a day.

poshtip

Black mussels may be collected from the rocks at low tide and are also cultivated and sold fresh and frozen. A few simple rules apply to safe mussel-eating. In tidal zones, collect from the deepest areas where they're further from the influence of shore pollution. More importantly, avoid areas which may be polluted, and watch for toxic tides.

poshquaffing

Phew! Garlic, ginger, chilli, lemon grass and coriander all conspire to challenge a vinous marriage. Gravitas is required and comes in the form of tropical tang from trendy viognier (usually oaked), or floral gewürztraminer in special late harvest style. Vanilla-oak infused chardonnay is a safe, if unimaginitve, haven.

Indonesian cuisine has a myriad tantalizing flavours, heady, haunting aromas, a kaleidoscope of colours and the overlay of textures. Contrasts create equilibrium; chilli quenched by cooling coconut, crisply fried sidekicks with a dish of rice, hot sambals to perk up milder dishes, gentle condiments to temper the heat of curry.

The phenomenal popularity of **pasta** is due to much
more than flavour, aroma and form. It has an innate sense
of honesty – it never sends out mixed messages – and
intervention by the cook to make it into anything
that it isn't has no hope of succeeding.

Which is enormously satisfying to those for whom prissy
presentation is anathema; it's physically impossible to coerce
noodles into landing anywhere other than where
they want to go! Buon appetito!

Pasta is the soul of generosity.

It enjoys being presented in large bowls

(sauce separate, tossed in, or spooned on top, you choose);

loves being passed round, scooped out and slithered onto a plate;

simply adores being a second helping.

It's absolute bliss to twirl your fork into a pile of steaming pasta and lift it towards waiting lips. And pasta is perfect for any mood, as it can be dressed up or down, depending on the occasion, how much time you've got, how much of your heard-earned cash you wish to spend – or how keen you are to impress your guests. The rest of the menu matters, too, so it's wise to think about that as well.

Pasta is arguably the most sensual thing you can cook, whether you've gone to the trouble of making it yourself or nipped out to the shop to buy a packet of good quality ready-made stuff.

Some say that Marco Polo discovered pasta in China and introduced it to Italy in 1295. Try telling that to the Italians! They claim the idea was theirs first and, if you've ever tangled with an Italian, you'll know better than to even broach the subject.

Enter the realms of fresh (home-made, egg-enriched, soft or dried) versus commercial pasta and things get really heated. Hard-core purists maintain that the only type worth eating is that which has been made by hand – a painstaking craft that should never be taken lightly, turned into a machine-manufactured thing, or in any other way put asunder.

Lesser mortals don't give two hoots for such niceties and reckon that pasta is pasta is pasta. Which, of course, it isn't! Most steer a middle course, making the dough if time and energy permit (and if they're the proud owners of a pasta-making machine), or investing in a good quality, rich egg pasta when they're feeling a trifle more picky, or when everything gets too much.

Whichever type you choose, here are a few pointers regarding the sensitive subject of saucing your pasta, a matter that has less to do with authenticity than being mindful of the integrity of the flavour and texture of everything from the pasta to the various components of the accompanying sauce.

Flour-and-water pastas like spaghetti are happiest with spicy, full-flavoured sauces based on olive oil. And, as they absorb sauces more readily, egg pastas prefer more gently flavoured cream-enriched sauces.

Bear in mind the shape of the noodles: flat pastas like tagliatelle, fettucine and pappardelle lap up creamy sauces that coat broad surfaces. Tubes like penne are best with dense sauces. Strands of long pasta like spaghetti and spaghettini wrap nicely around bulky, textured sauces.

These pearls of wisdom will make your own pasta-making endeavours more successful, and your visits to Italian restaurants less fraught with tension. Though the chef may politely do your bidding and serve penne with a creamy alfredo sauce or fettucine with a herbed tomato mix, cross-dressing his carefully mix-and-matched menu may injure his innermost soul.

posh pasta tips, hints, facts and foibles

➤ Good quality pasta is made from hard durum wheat that ensures that pasta has a superior taste, texture and colour, and keeps its shape when cooked. Soft wheat produces pasta that cooks up sadly soft and soggy.

➤ Allow about 100g of dried pasta per person; a little extra if you're serving a light sauce; less if the sauce is rich and creamy.

➤ Use lots of water, but don't drown it! 1 litre per 100g with 7ml (1½ teaspoons) salt is about right. A dash of oil helps keeps the strands separate and the pot from boiling over. Add the pasta all at once when the water is boiling rapidly, pressing the strands gently until completely submerged. Cover the pot to speed up the return to the boil, then uncover while the pasta cooks.

➤ Purists prefer their pasta cooked *al dente* ('to the tooth'). The only way to test is by biting it. The instant your pearly whites meet with minimum resistance, tip the pasta into a colander, give it a couple of firm shakes, and tip into a warm bowl. Toss with a dash of olive oil.

➤ For obvious reasons never cook two types of pasta at the same time. The cooking time varies from type to type and, even more so, between home-made and commercial pasta.

➤ Be sparing with the sauce. An overdose will ruin the distinctive flavour and texture of the pasta. Offer olive oil as well if you wish.

➤ A scattering of parmesan cheese is obligatory (except with seafood pastas, when it's a no-no), if possible brought to the table in a block to be shaved or grated on the spot.

➤ The correct way to eat pasta is with a fork. Use the side of the bowl to keep things manageable; if you twirl it into the bowl of your spoon, any watching Italian will sob salt tears.

➤ Never, ever cut the strands with your knife, or bite them off in mid-air. If you can't manage it, have ravioli instead!

spaghetti, melty cheese
and herb-zapped tomatoes

In this easy, no-fuss dish, the sauce is ready by the time the pasta is cooked. But, with all recipes that are bared down to the basics, the quality of the ingredients is vital, so go out of your way to source the very best. And don't even think about using tinned tomatoes; only fresh, ripe ones will do.

serves 4 to 6

800g ripe tomatoes, blanched, peeled and cut into tiny dice (see page 63)
100g full-cream mozzarella cheese, cut into small cubes
1 wheel feta cheese, crumbled
24 calamata olives, stoned and sliced
125ml (½ cup) chopped herbs (flat-leaf parsley, basil, oregano, marjoram, thyme)
sea salt and milled black pepper
80ml (⅓ cup) olive oil
500g spaghetti
shaved parmesan cheese, for garnishing

Put the tomatoes, mozzarella, feta, olives and herbs into a serving bowl large enough to accommodate the pasta. Season generously with salt and pepper. Warm the olive oil in a small saucepan until it's smoking hot, pour over and mix in well.

Cook the pasta in a large saucepan of salted, boiling water. Drain well in a colander, then tip it into the ingredients in the bowl and toss everything together. Cover the bowl with a plate and set aside for about 2 minutes until the cheese melts.

to serve Pile the pasta into bowls and garnish generously with shaved parmesan cheese.

makeahead
The joy of this recipe is that it takes only a couple of minutes to prepare once the ingredients are ready.

poshtip
Spaghetti is one of the long pastas that include spaghettini, angel hair, linguine, bucatini and fusilli longhi, all of which are perfect for this recipe.

poshquaffing
The racy ingredients suggest a Mediterranean red but, once melded into the finished ensemble, simple white wine wins the toss. A quality entry-level dry white – chenin blanc based with generous fruit – provides an unobtrusive stage on which the ripe flavours play out. Without clanking competition.

fresh herbs have been used for medicinal purposes from the year dot, and much of what was previously considered magic has been proved by scientific analysis and transcribed into herbal remedies. Since the Middle Ages herbs have been used to flavour food, a vogue that has reached its full expression on today's table. Fresh herbs are pivotal to the flavours in this recipe, so don't substitute dried herbs. You're welcome to use your favourites (even if they aren't the ones specified); just be generous with the amount.

Tomatoes are easy to peel. Simply cut a cross in the bottom with a sharp knife, then plunge into a pan of boiling water. Leave for about 10 seconds (a little longer if they aren't fully ripe), then lift from the water and peel away the skins. Gently squeeze out the seeds and chop the tomatoes as required for the recipe.

taglierini with green peas
and pancetta crisps

Peas and ham have had a longer culinary relationship than most ingredients I know – homely pea and ham soup is a case in point. Here they join forces to tizzy up a bowl of pasta and turn it into a thing of beauty. Any of the ribbon pastas like tagliatelle and fettucine may be used in this recipe.

serves 4

8 slices pancetta
vegetable or olive oil
250ml (1 cup) vegetable stock or chicken stock (page 15)
125ml (½ cup) dry white wine
250ml (1 cup) cream
250ml (1 cup) fresh or frozen green peas
30ml (2 tablespoons) chopped sage leaves
4–5 spring onions, trimmed and finely sliced
sea salt and milled black pepper
300g taglierini

Fry the pancetta in a dash of oil in a non-stick frying pan until crispy. Drain well on paper towel, then crumble roughly.

Combine the stock and wine in a medium saucepan and boil uncovered until reduced by half. Add the cream and boil uncovered until the sauce thickens slightly. Add the peas, sage and spring onions and simmer for about a minute, just long enough to heat everything through. You don't want the peas turning khaki! Check the flavour and season with salt and pepper.

Just before serving, cook the pasta in a large saucepan of salted, boiling water. Drain well and pile into a warm bowl. Pour the sauce on top, and toss gently to mix.

to serve Scoop the pasta into deep, warm bowls and top with crumbled pancetta. A couple of sage leaves won't go amiss either.

makeahead

Cook the sauce to the half-way stage a day ahead. Stop after reducing the stock, wine and cream and before adding the peas. Refrigerate until shortly before serving, then finish everything off in a flash.

poshquaffing

Racy sauvignon blanc lifts the earthy duo of peas and bacon interleaved with a rich herb sauce, but risks standing apart. Gently dry rosé or blanc de noir is a better bet: the ochre colour adds elegance, berry fruit and a tinge of sweetness supporting fullness. Red wines obtrude, with the exception of cherry-berry pinot noir.

peas are the prettiest of vegetables, and there are many different types available, all suitable for this recipe. Petit pois (small peas), a dwarf variety, are harvested when they're young and innocent, and shelled before cooking. Mangetout (also known as snow peas or sugarsnap peas) are eaten whole in the pod. Garden peas (simply called green peas) are seldom available fresh, so it's lucky that frozen peas are such a good alternative; the freezing process doesn't seem to bother them too much, and flavour and texture are well maintained. Don't use tinned peas unless you aren't fazed by khaki-coloured pasta sauce.

Culinary overkill is anathema to a meal; the dictum 'less is more' rules, which is abundantly clear in this simple recipe where the charm lies solely on a few perfect ingredients.

tagliatelle with smoked salmon
in fennel lemon cream

This luxurious pasta is quick and easy to prepare – perfect for lunch, light dinner or even served as a half-portion for a starter. Any of the ribbon pastas are perfect, including fettucine and taglierini. If your budget won't stretch to smoked salmon, less costly trout will do almost as well.

serves 4

500ml (2 cups) fish stock or vegetable stock (page 15)
250ml (1 cup) cream
finely grated zest and juice of ½ lemon (approximate amount)
200g thinly sliced smoked salmon
30ml (2 tablespoons) chopped fennel
sea salt and milled black pepper
400g tagliatelle
olive oil
50g fish roe, for garnishing (optional)

Bring the stock, cream and lemon zest and juice to the boil in a medium saucepan. Boil uncovered, stirring occasionally, until the sauce is sufficiently reduced to coat the spoon.

Add the salmon and fennel and heat through. Check the flavour and season with salt and pepper, and a squish more lemon juice if necessary.

At the last possible moment, cook the pasta in a large saucepan of salted boiling water. Drain well in a colander, then tip into a warm bowl. Add a dash of olive oil and toss.

to serve Lift the pasta into warm bowls and top with sauce. Garnish with fish roe and fennel fronds if you have a couple handy.

makeahead

This is easy to prepare once all the ingredients are sorted out. For even simpler serving, though, reduce the stock, cream and lemon zest and juice a couple of hours ahead, and chill it in the fridge. Finishing the dish is then quick-as-a-lick.

posh**tips**

To trim the cost, use smoked trout instead of smoked salmon. And instead of fish roe, garnish with roasted, chopped hazelnuts.

posh**quaffing**

Brimming with oil-rich fish, sultry smoke, singular fennel and salty roe, this pasta begs for contrast. Linear, focussed, grassy sauvignon blanc provides the tart lance to 'cut' the sauce and freshen the palate. Sylvaner's waxy spice is a fuller alternative; red wines are best left on the rack.

smoked salmon   'belongs to gastronomy's aristocracy and so is prone to counterfeit' to quote the late, great gourmet, Peter Devereux. Most salmon for smoking comes from the Pacific coasts of Canada and Alaska or from a Norwegian salmon farm. Smoked trout (a river fish) is something else entirely which, in turn, is different from 'salmon trout' (sea-water fish farmed in fresh water with colouring added to the feed to make the flesh pink). Although salmon and trout belong to the same family, they're not able to interbreed, so there's no such thing as a salmon trout.

spaghettini
with rocket and coriander pesto

Pesto always brings to mind languid summer meals, because it's usually made with basil, a fragrant herb at its best in warmer months. Our snappy version uses rocket mixed with coriander, which is tossed into hot pasta. And instead of costly pine nuts, peanuts are a satisfactory substitute for those of us with half an eye on the purse strings.

serves 4 to 5

rocket and coriander pesto
60g rocket leaves
60g coriander (stalks and leaves)
2 garlic cloves, peeled
100g salted and roasted peanuts
125ml (½ cup) olive oil (or half olive, half vegetable oil)
25g grated parmesan cheese

400g spaghettini or spaghetti
sea salt and milled black pepper
olive oil
shaved parmesan cheese, for garnishing

rocket and coriander pesto Pound the rocket, coriander, garlic and nuts together with a pestle and mortar (or in a food processor) to form a paste. Mix in the oil, then add the cheese. If using a food processor, take care that you don't over-mix or you'll spoil the slightly rough texture. Check the flavour and season with salt and pepper.

Shortly before serving, cook the pasta in a large saucepan of salted boiling water. Drain well in a colander, then tip into a bowl. Season with salt and pepper, and toss with olive oil and the pesto. Use your hands; it's far easier that way.

to serve Lift the pasta into wide-brimmed plates and garnish generously with grated parmesan.

pesto is traditionally made with a pestle and mortar, a gadget that has made a come-back thanks to television chefs favouring it over mechanised blenders. Besides being bliss with pasta, pesto may be piled onto salty biscuits at snacking hour, plopped into Indonesian-style seafood soup (page 56), or stirred into mayonnaise (page 102) to accompany smoked fish or as a topping for grilled or barbecued steak.

makeahead
Pesto keeps well in the fridge for a couple of days and may be frozen quite successfully. In this case omit the cheese, salt and pepper and add just before serving.

poshquaffing
Southern Rhone-styled red blends are capturing increasing shelf space. Shiraz-based, often with grenache, carignan and other exotica, they're perfect partners for pesto, more so when rocket and coriander add their inimitible zest. The only white wine that will cope, if you insist, is a fruity, off-dry chenin blanc.

tagliatelle, braised butternut
and roasted pumpkin seeds

All the ingredients for this soul-soothing creation are usually on hand, so you don't have to nip
down to the shop before whipping it up. Butternut and tomatoes perk up each other no end,
and roasted pumpkin seeds lend a surprisingly good crunch at the end.

serves 4 to 5

50g butter
1 small onion, very finely chopped
1 medium butternut (about 500g), skinned, pipped and cut into small dice
2 ripe tomatoes, blanched, peeled and chopped (see page 63)
leaves from 1 long sprig thyme
250ml (1 cup) vegetable stock or chicken stock (page 15)
sea salt and milled black pepper
250ml (1 cup) cream
400g tagliatelle
100g pumpkin seeds, roasted in a dry frying pan

Heat the butter in a large frying pan and fry the onion until golden. Add the butternut and stir it
around for a couple of minutes until well coloured and slightly softened, and has absorbed the
delicious flavours of the oniony butter.

Add the tomato, thyme leaves and stock, season with salt and pepper and simmer uncovered
until reduced by half. Add the cream and continue cooking for a few minutes more until the
sauce thickens slightly and the butternut is tender. Check the flavour and adjust it if necessary.

Just before serving, cook the pasta in a large saucepan of salted boiling water. Drain well in
a colander, then tip into a warm bowl.

to serve Heap the pasta into warm bowls, top with butternut sauce and garnish with a handful
of roasted pumpkin seeds.

makeahead

Braised butternut sauce reheats
perfectly; keep covered and
refrigerated for up to two days.

poshtip

All the ribbon pastas – like tagliatelle,
taglierini, pappardelle and fettucine –
work best with creamy sauces like this
one, so choose your favourite.

poshquaffing

Chardonnay, billed as the ultimate
food wine yet often too trenchant
to play a supporting act, finally has
its day. The butternut's flavour is
enhanced in the frying, and the
pumpkin seeds by roasting, so a
full (not over-wooded) chardonnay
is a prime partner. Red wine adherents
may find solace in a low-tannin
ruby cabernet.

pumpkin doesn't have to remain stuck in the foody doldrums forever; it may be flossied up in all manner of posh
ways, this yummy recipe being just one of them. And pumpkin seeds aren't just good to crunch; they are hugely
nutritious and believed to preserve virility and ward off prostate problems.

My darling dad called pasta 'travelling food' as it can be eaten anywhere you're comfortable. So we photographed his favourite pasta on his old travelling chest that accompanied him on many ocean cruises to far-flung places.

mushroom pappardelle
with gorgonzola cream

Mushrooms and gorgonzola were made for each other. Here they create a luxurious pasta sauce, where bags of fresh parsley adds its own special charm. Tagliatelle may be substituted for pappardelle if you wish.

serves 4 to 5

butter and vegetable oil
1 small onion, finely sliced
200g mushrooms, sliced (mix wild and cultivated for the best flavour)
250ml (1 cup) cream
50g gorgonzola or blue cheese, crumbled
small bunch flat-leaf parsley, chopped
sea salt and milled black pepper
400g pappardelle
shaved or grated parmesan cheese, for garnishing

Heat a little butter and oil in a medium frying pan and lightly fry the onion until golden and richly flavoured. Add the mushrooms, cover and sweat over gentle heat for about 3 minutes until they sweat and soften. Add the cream, cheese and half the parsley, and boil uncovered for a few minutes until the sauce thickens just a little. Check the flavour and season with salt and pepper.

When your guests are ready and waiting, cook the pasta in a large saucepan of salted boiling water. Drain well in a colander. Tip the pasta into the sauce and toss everything together.

to serve Scoop the pasta onto warm plates and scatter over the remaining parsley. Allow everyone to add as much grated or shaved parmesan as their heart desires.

makeahead

The mushroom and gorgonzola sauce may be prepared up to a day ahead. Reheat, and cook the pasta just before serving.

poshtip

Fresh sage is delicious in this dish, so feel free to add a handful of finely shredded leaves when stirring in the chopped parsley.

poshquaffing

Local versions of Pineau des Charentes, a *vin de liqueur* of France's Cognac region, are few and far between, but well worth seeking out for this extravaganza. Served cool, the fruity, sweet grape flavour and fortifying alcohol amply escort earthy mushrooms and creamy blue cheese. Light red muscadel is a more prevalent alternative.

dried mushrooms add a distinctive flavour to this dish, and you're welcome to use them instead of (or as well as) fresh fungi. Soak 20g dried porcini mushrooms in a cupful of lukewarm water for about 20 minutes to plump. Drain in a fine strainer set over a bowl and press out the liquor. Chop the mushrooms coarsely, then add to the sauce with the liquor.

When snooping about in pine forests for wild mushrooms, you need sturdy walking shoes, a probing stick and plenty of patience. Not to mention the skill of knowing the difference between edible mushrooms and their poisonous cousins!

penne
with slow-cooked peperonata

Peperonata (tomato heaven), full of rich, unctuous flavour, is the mother of all pasta partners. Mix various tomato types for depth of flavour, and ensure that they're fully ripe and bursting with flavour.

serves 4 to 6

olive oil
2 anchovy fillets, drained and chopped
1 large onion, sliced
4 garlic cloves, peeled and crushed
1 red or yellow pepper, cored and sliced
750g ripe plum tomatoes, blanched, peeled and roughly chopped (see page 63),
   or 400g tin tomatoes, chopped in their sauce
300g ripe cocktail tomatoes, halved
125ml (½ cup) dry red wine
60ml (4 tablespoons) chopped herbs (flat-leaf parsley, oregano, thyme)
100g stoned calamata olives
small bunch basil leaves, roughly torn
sea salt, milled black pepper, sugar
400g penne
grated or shaved parmesan cheese, for garnishing

Heat a little olive oil in a frying pan. Add the anchovy and warm gently, mashing it into the oil. Add the onion, garlic and pepper, cover and cook over medium heat until the vegetables are nice and soft.

Stir in the tomatoes, wine and chopped herbs, cover and cook for about 30 minutes, stirring occasionally, until the sauce is nice and mushy. Add the olives and basil, season with pepper, and heat through. Check the flavour and add a little sugar and salt if necessary – but bear in mind that anchovy is salty.

At the very last minute cook the penne in a large saucepan of salted boiling water. Drain well in a colander, then tip into a warm serving bowl.

to serve Offer the pasta, peperonata and grated or shaved parmesan cheese separately so that everyone can help themselves to as much as they like.

makeahead

No problem at all. Make the sauce up to two days ahead, chill in the fridge, and reheat at the last minute. Cook the pasta just before serving.

poshtip

If a touch of heat turns you on, be my guest – chop up a couple of fresh red or green chillies and add to the peperonata.

poshquaffing

Anchovy amplifies the invigorating peperonata and, with tomato, wine and herbs, conjures up images of Italy. Go 'Italian' on a local scale in search of a match: increasing plantings of sangiovese, nebbiolo and barbera are finding their way into Med-red blends, which are made for this dish. Pinotage or zinfandel are willing substitutes.

After an alluring starter and as a precursor to a

seductive pud, the main course is the Big Event.

I'm talking about an in-your-face,

drop-dead gorgeous moment,

a culinary highlight of epic proportions

in terms of comely looks and tempting taste.

As part of a posh menu, Mains needs to be way

different from food cobbled together for hungry moments,

which is often more about expedience than artistry.

A posh main course is not about quantity. A hunk of meat, a stodgy starch and a couple of vegetables is a strange concept in many cultures, and there's lots to be said for replacing one main dish with an array served buffet-style (or placed casually on the table), or a tasting menu consisting of a tempting assortment of smaller portions.

Feeling full has to do with losing interest in flavour, so there's something to be said for both trains of thought. Besides which, the meal takes longer, and if you've gone to the pleasurable trouble of having invited friends round for a meal, you're entitled to enjoy their company for as long as possible.

For many, meat is the be-all and end-all of any meal. Don't entirely agree; I'm a pushover for a cunningly created non-meat dish. More importantly when all is said, done and fulsomely enjoyed, what is served with the main event – sauces, accompaniments and suchlike – often steals your heart away.

From the moment cooks showed vegetables a modicum of respect (and stopped overcooking them), they came out of the closet and started making their considerable presence felt. And despite the occasional grumble from committed carnivores, there's a swing towards meat-free meals. Vegetables, pulses, grains and noodles are increasingly playing starring roles in their own right – at home and on restaurant menus.

Their upswing in popularity is due to various factors: veggies are good for you, plus there's more on offer than ever, the quality and variety is superb, and they're pocket-friendly. Remember, creativity knows no bounds – if you can dream it, you can cook it.

If you have the choice, shop for vegetables grown locally: the time span between picking and cooking is shorter and they'll be way more nutritious and delicious. In the interests of taste, texture and goodness, buy organic produce that isn't shrouded in plastic. Look for the brightest, perkiest, lushest and most fragrant among the offerings and leave the rest behind for cooks less finicky than you are.

The meat-free recipes in this section focus on freshness, texture and flavour. You'll notice a few timely twists and tweaks, juxtaposing flavour, texture and colour to tease the taste buds and please the eye, while still retaining the basic goodness and integrity of each ingredient.

Feel free to serve a salad on the side. But what makes a good one? Some would say the dressing; then again others, the quality and variety of the ingredients. Truth is, something in between; a lousy dressing will spoil the best salad, and ingredients past their prime won't be helped by the most artfully-mixed dressing. There are loads of ideas on page 21.

It's no longer cool to tear up a crisphead lettuce and bury it in a store-bought dressing. Vary the leaves to add interest, seeking out soft butter lettuce, cos, little gems, endive, radicchio (red chicory), oak-leaf and red lettuce. More unusual 'designer leaves' that find their way into salads include rocket, mizuna, watercress, young beetroot leaves and infant spinach.

Jettison outer leaves if they're less than perfect, remove the centre core of crisp lettuces with your thumb (cutting with a knife or scissors will cause leaves to turn brown), separate the leaves of soft lettuces and soak in plenty of cold water. Drain, spin dry and store on a wad of kitchen paper in an airtight container.

Add garnishes like croûtons (page 43), crumbled feta, crisp bean sprouts and roasted nuts and seeds for crunch. I love a salad with a sting of onion in it, but don't just wallop in any old brown onion – instead choose sweeter and more mildly flavoured red onion, finely sliced leeks, shallots or spring onions.

aromatic noodle stir-fry
with sesame-toasted tofu

serves 4

200g dried egg noodles or rice noodles
20ml (4 teaspoons) sesame oil
3–4 spring onions, trimmed and finely sliced
1 red or yellow pepper, cored and very finely sliced
15ml (1 tablespoon) scraped and finely chopped fresh ginger
60ml (4 tablespoons) soy sauce
10ml (2 teaspoons) fish sauce
10ml (2 teaspoons) brown sugar
30g rocket leaves
30ml (2 tablespoons) shredded mint leaves
30ml (2 tablespoons) shredded basil leaves
30ml (2 tablespoons) sesame seeds, roasted in a dry frying pan

sesame-toasted tofu
100g firm tofu
1 egg white, lightly beaten
125ml (½ cup) sesame seeds
vegetable oil

Pour boiling water over the noodles in a bowl and set aside for about 2 minutes to soften. Drain well in a colander.

Heat the sesame oil in medium frying pan, add the spring onions and pepper, and stir-fry until softened. Add the ginger, soy sauce, fish sauce and brown sugar, then stir in the drained noodles, rocket, mint and basil. Stir-fry until the rocket is limp and everything is piping hot.

sesame-toasted tofu Slice the tofu into batons, dip in egg white, then roll in sesame seeds. Heat a little vegetable oil in a non-stick frying pan and fry the tofu on all sides until the seeds have crisped; this should only take a minute or two.

to serve Pile the hot noodles into bowls, top with sesame-toasted tofu and scatter over the roasted sesame seeds. Serve immediately.

tofu, also known as soy bean curd, is made from ground, cooked soy beans. It seems rather bland and characterless, yet tastes slightly nutty and has the happy knack of taking on the flavours of the dish it's in. The good news is that it's high in protein and cholesterol free.

makeahead

Prepare all the ingredients and sizzle this dish up just before you serve it; it loses all its appeal if it has to stand around for any length of time.

poshtip

Choose firm tofu for cooking; soft, silken tofu is far too fragile. Store uncooked tofu in the fridge for up to a week, covered with water. Change the water daily.

poshquaffing

Soy in various forms – bean curd and sauce – with sesame suggests rice wine, but its mouth-puckering medicinal character overwhelms. A flinty dry white based on either of the rieslings – 'Cape' or the real McCoy – keep the palate fresh. The mousse of decent bubbly also lifts this oriental dish.

Visits to Hong Kong have instilled a love for — and understanding of — noodle dishes, and inspired this recipe. While taking more than a couple of liberties in terms of mixing western and oriental ingredients, it's everything that excellent Chinese cuisine should be: a harmony of colour, flavour and texture.

east african lentil rice
with soft borrie maize meal

Eating in East Africa – Mozambique, Tanzania, Kenya – is a unique experience, shaped by local ingredients and spices. Meat is usually reserved for special occasions, so vegetables, beans and lentil dishes are extremely popular.

serves 8 to 10

125ml (½ cup) brown lentils
375ml (1½ cups) cold water
50g butter
1 cinnamon stick
5ml (1 teaspoon) cumin seeds
2ml (½ teaspoon) turmeric (borrie)
2ml (½ teaspoon) ground ginger
1ml (¼ teaspoon) ground cardamom
1ml (¼ teaspoon) ground cloves
1 onion, finely chopped
5ml (1 teaspoon) sea salt
250ml (1 cup) brown rice
500ml (2 cups) boiling water
250ml (1 cup) fresh or frozen green peas
4 hard-boiled eggs (optional)
coriander leaves, for garnishing
soft borrie maize meal, to serve (page 152)

Rinse the lentils in cold water, drain well in a colander, then tip into a small saucepan. Add the cold water, cover and simmer for 15 minutes. Drain well.

Heat the butter in a medium saucepan. Stir in the cinnamon, cumin, turmeric, ginger, cardamom and cloves, and sizzle for about 10 seconds until the spices are lightly roasted and smell divine. Stir in the onion and salt, cover and sweat gently for 3 minutes until the onion is translucent. Add the lentils, rice and boiling water, cover and simmer for about 25 minutes until the rice and lentils are tender and the liquid has been absorbed.

Just before serving, add the peas (defrost first if they're frozen) and heat through; this is all the time they need to cook.

to serve Pile the lentil rice onto a serving plate and garnish with quartered hard-boiled eggs and a profusion of coriander leaves. Serve with soft borrie maize meal.

makeahead

Make this dish a day or two ahead, but don't add the peas, as they tend to discolour. Cover and chill in the fridge, and bring to room temperature before adding the peas and reheating very gently in a saucepan on the stove-top, or covered in a hot oven.

poshtip

If you want the yolks to stay in the centre of hard-boiled eggs, stir the water as they cook to keep them turning in the egg white.

poshquaffing

Tempered by heat, the spices are far less hectic than the dry ingredients suggest. Riesling's scents embroider those of the pot, but its gentility is coshed by the food's fullness of flavour. Easy shiraz appeals until the tannins muscle through the savoury crowd. Best is oaked sauvignon blanc: the creamy texture buffs the patina of spice.

roasted brinjal boats
with tomato, feta and olives

Brinjals, stars of Mediterranean cuisine, are succulent, full-flavoured and packed with attitude. Who needs meat when a vegetable can deliver all this? This dish is perfect served at room temperature at a long, lazy lunch.

serves 4 as a starter or side dish; 2 as a main course

2 medium brinjals
olive oil
12 cocktail tomatoes, halved or quartered
1 wheel feta cheese, crumbled
60ml (4 tablespoons) crème fraîche
15ml (1 tablespoon) drained capers
8 green olives, stoned and chopped
60ml (4 tablespoons) chopped flat-leaf parsley
4 large basil leaves, finely shredded
sea salt and milled black pepper
125ml (½ cup) grated parmesan cheese

Slice the brinjals lengthwise and use a spoon to hollow out the centres, leaving a border around the edges. Brush the brinjal shells liberally with olive oil and place in a baking dish. Heat the oven to 180°C.

Chop the brinjal flesh and mix in the tomatoes, feta, crème fraîche, capers, olives, parsley and basil. Season with salt and pepper. Fill the brinjal boats, piling it high as the filling will sink as it cooks. Scatter parmesan cheese on top.

Cover the baking dish with foil and bake the brinjals for 60 minutes. Remove the foil, increase the heat to 200°C and roast for about 10 minutes more to brown the cheese. Serve hot or cool.

makeahead

This dish tastes great hot from the oven or after it has cooled down. To make life even easier, get it ready for roasting a day ahead. Cover and chill in the meanwhile.

poshquaffing

The inherent lanolin creaminess of semillon, boosted by clean wood, is a sturdy foil for the sunny Med components, and echoes the earthy brinjal flavour. Athletic Bordeaux varieties – cabernet franc, malbec and petit verdot – offer a red alternative, but if you serve a big fat shiraz, you'll ruin the thing completely.

brinjals, a voluptuous mixture of earthiness and tenderness, originated in tropical Asia and have a meatiness quite unlike any other vegetable. They have many names; Britain adopted the French *aubergine*, a name that has its origins in Sanskrit *vatin-ganah* ('anti-wind'), through Persian *badin-gan*, Arabic *al-badinjan* and Catalan *alberginera*, which neatly tracks its culinary history. Eggplant, its American title, is in deference to it's shape, though this varies, as does the colour which can range from white, whitish-green, dark green to yellow and the more familiar deep purplish-black.

Food – and its preparation and presentation – should be a pleasure. If it looks good in the baking dish, serve it in that.

maize meal tart
with country vegetables

Portuguese traders brought Indian corn (maize) to Africa from America many centuries ago, never dreaming of how many ways it would be enjoyed at the southern tip of the continent, where it's fondly known as 'pap'. Here it forms a base for an unctuous filling of mushrooms, tomato and onion. It looks good and tastes even better.

serves 8

butter, for greasing the pan
750ml (3 cups) vegetable stock (page 15)
250ml (1 cup) maize meal
2ml (½ teaspoon) sea salt
30g (2 tablespoons) butter
50g grated gruyère or cheddar cheese
2 egg yolks

country vegetables
1 onion, thickly sliced
olive oil
250g cocktail tomatoes
4 large black mushrooms, sliced
leaves from 2–3 long sprigs thyme, plus extra for garnishing
sea salt and milled black pepper
125ml (½ cup) stoned calamata olives

Butter a 22cm quiche tin. Bring the stock to the boil in a medium saucepan. Tip in the maize meal and salt, and stir over high heat for about 3 minutes until it thickens. Remove from the heat and beat in the butter, then the cheese and egg yolks. Set aside to cool.

Heat the oven to 200ºC. Line the quiche tin with maize meal as evenly as possible, pressing it with your fingers onto the base and up the sides. Bake uncovered for about 40 minutes until crisp and golden.

country vegetables Lightly brown the onion in a little olive oil in a frying pan. Add the tomatoes, mushrooms and thyme, and season with salt and pepper. Cover and steam gently for about 5 minutes until tender. Spoon the vegetables into the warm tart case, scatter the olives on top and garnish gaily with thyme sprigs.

to serve Remove the tart from the baking tin, place on a large plate and serve warm. A simple green salad on the side is all that's needed for a sesnational meat-free meal.

makeahead

The tart case doesn't mind being prepared ahead and refrigerated for a day. Reheat in a low oven. Cook the vegetables and fill the tart shortly before serving.

poshtips

If you prefer, use polenta instead of maize meal. And remember to store it in a well-sealed container, preferably in the fridge, to prevent infestation by bugs or other unwelcome goggas.

poshquaffing

Pinotage, either alone or in new wave 'Cape blends', delivers just enough pithy berry fruit and savoury spice for the topping, and is a natural parochial partner for 'pap'. Meaty merlot with smoky scents of oak is more retiring, while zinfandel offers both girth and an Italian connection: it originated there as primitivo.

indian paneer
with rocket and roasted tomatoes

East meets West in this spicy fusion dish with loads of colour and zingy flavours. The best Indian recipes are brimming with gentle spices and evocative heat, a far cry from burning curries prepared by less sensitive cooks. Here perfectly spiced home-made paneer (fresh cheese) acts as a catalyst to unctuous tomato and rocket. Serve solo with curried or plain vegetables, or as a partner to fish or chicken.

serves 4

olive oil
4–5 large, ripe roma tomatoes, thickly sliced
sugar, sea salt, milled black pepper
60g rocket leaves

paneer
2 litres (8 cups) full cream milk
60ml (4 tablespoons) freshly squeezed lemon juice
1 large onion, finely chopped
vegetable oil
1 green chilli, seeded and finely chopped
2ml (½ teaspoon) sea salt
2ml (½ teaspoon) garam masala or roasted masala (page 24)
2ml (½ teaspoon) turmeric (borrie)
2ml (½ teaspoon) ground coriander
2ml (½ teaspoon) cumin seeds
50g roasted and salted cashew nuts

Heat the oven to 180°C. Line a baking tray with foil and brush (or spray) with olive oil. Lay the tomato slices on top, season with sugar, salt and pepper, and roast for about 30 minutes until semi-dried. Keep warm.

paneer Bring the milk to the boil in a saucepan, add the lemon juice, then remove from the heat. Stir until the curds separate from the whey, then drain in a colander lined with muslin or a double layer of 'kitchen wipes'. Cover and set aside for an hour or two for the whey to run off. Squeeze out the excess moisture, tip the paneer into a bowl and break it up gently with a fork.

Fry the onion in a little oil in a frying pan until golden. Add the chilli, salt, masala, turmeric, coriander and cumin, and fry for about 30 seconds. Add the nuts. Toss the onion gently with the paneer, taking care not to mush everything up too much.

to serve Scoop spoonfuls of paneer onto a foil-lined tray and place under the oven grill until well browned. Arrange the rocket leaves on a large platter or individual plates. Top with roasted tomatoes and grilled paneer. Serve warm.

makeahead
Tomatoes may be roasted, paneer prepared and rocket leaves washed and dried a day ahead. Reheat the tomatoes, grill the paneer and assemble the dish at the last moment.

poshtip
If you're really not into the mood to make your own paneer, use ricotta cheese instead.

poshquaffing
It would have to be some wine to simultaneously carry the fresh cheese and smooth the coriander, cumin and chilli. Chardonnay does the trick, in fulll flavoured oaked form. The breadth of flavour matches the dish and a citric zing lifts the tail. Experiments with cooled fruity reds are ongoing, without success.

Your main course doesn't have to have been born with fins, trotters or hoofs. If the recipe is interesting enough, it will please all comers.

caponata
on maize meal wedges

Besides being a hit vegetarian item on crisp maize meal wedges, caponata is great with roast meats or smoked fish, and the perfect with assorted cheeses, bread, olives and suchlike. The aromatic mélange needs to be perfect in both texture and colour; don't chop the vegetables too small and never overcook them to mushy anonymity. Purists use just parsley and basil for flavour, but you may enjoy adding other freshly plucked herbs as well.

serves 6

maize meal wedges (page 152)

caponata
1 brinjal, cut into chunks (skin on)
sea salt and milled black pepper
olive oil
2 large onions, thickly sliced
4 garlic cloves, peeled and crushed
2 red or yellow peppers, cored and cut into large chunks
4 large, ripe tomatoes, skinned and quartered (see page 63)
60ml (4 tablespoons) chopped flat-leaf parsley
sugar, paprika
60ml (4 tablespoons) shredded basil leaves

Prepare the maize meal wedges ready for grilling.

caponata Pile the brinjal chunks into a colander, sprinkle with salt and set aside for about 15 minutes. Rinse and pat dry. (Salting first means they'll brown better and absorb less oil.)

Heat a little olive oil in a large saucepan and fry the onion until golden. Add the garlic, brinjals, peppers, tomatoes and parsley, and season with salt, pepper, sugar and paprika. Cover and simmer for about 10 minutes until the vegetables are tender. Stir in the basil.

If there's too much liquid, transfer the vegetables to a serving bowl and boil the sauce uncovered until reduced and thickened slightly. Pour over the vegetables.

to serve Grill the maize meal wedges, place on warm plates, top with caponata and serve hot.

makeahead
Caponata is even better after a day or two when the flavours have had time to mingle and marry. Maize meal wedges are made in two stages, so make a day ahead and slice, butter and grill them shortly before serving. Keep everything refrigerated in the meanwhile.

poshtip
When shopping for brinjals, choose those with a tight, satiny skins. As a rule of thumb, the smaller the sweeter, though it's a good idea to select a size and shape best suited to the recipe.

poshquaffing
Maize meal and caponata signals for a versatile conductor. Fully flavoured, fruity chenin blanc answers the call, shepherding all into harmony. Touches of residual sweetness even enhance the outcome, but avoid wooded versions as there's no space for extra vanilla, or tannins.

There's no reason for vegetarians to feel short-changed when it comes to meat-free recipes. This one, for example, will have committed carnivors converting without a backward glance.

Marrying into a fishing-mad family and visiting fish markets all over the world – Tokyo, Singapore, New Orleans, Fremantle, Mauritius, Zanzibar – turned me on and tuned me in to the pleasures of catching, cooking (and eating) great seafood. It also resulted in my first cookbook, *Free From The Sea*, first published in 1979 and still going strong.

I was born to be a hunter-gatherer. My sisters and I would catch tadpoles in ponds on our little farm in the Fish Hoek valley. We kept them in jars, and watched in awe as they sprouted legs, turned into frogs and hopped away. Our dad taught us to catch klippies in the rock pools along the 'Catwalk' alongside the beach. But I don't suppose this counts, because we never actually ate the tadpoles, and always let the klippies go free.

Seaside holidays at Cape Infanta especially, are times when we're lucky enough to indulge in seafood of all types. Brunch generally consists of plump, wild oysters done every which way, from *au naturel* and washed down, as tradition dictates, with black velvet, to topped with crisply-crumbled pancetta and gently warmed over the dying embers of last night's fire.

We snack on black mussels simmered in their own juices and a dash of white wine, and periwinkles that we poach, prise with a pin from their shells, marinate briefly in vinaigrette and pile onto salty biscuits. A dab of crème fraîche is optional.

Later, when the fishermen return with a mixed bag of linefish – roman, grunter, kob and stumpnose – it's time to stoke up the coals for action. Fish are laid out for everyone to prepare their own favourite meal. Herbs are plucked and stuffed into cavities, the fish is then wrapped in foil and baked. Others may prefer their catch butterflied, brushed with olive oil and rubbed with a mix of warm Cape Malay spices – coriander, cardamom, black pepper, turmeric and cumin, and roasted to crisp perfection. No side dish required; just a glass of well-chilled chardonnay.

Fish fresh and free is always a bonus. Sardine runs on Hout Bay beach reward us with a feast of glistening tiddlers that would have gladdened the hearts of Strandlopers, early inhabitants of the southern African coast who once lived off aquatic pickings and precious little else.

Some sardines meet their demise in the freezer, wrapped cuddle-close and ready to bait our fishing hooks. Others are readied for the barbecue. Drop-of-the-hat dinner guests arrive and a satisfying sizzle assails the senses as the fish are grilled. Accompaniment? Shallots, garlic and butter wrapped in foil and roasted in the coals. To die for!

When shopping for seafood, it's essential to know what's what. For instance, linefish refers to pelagic fish (which live in the open sea; usually near the surface) and gamefish (pelagic fish with the fighting spirit that anglers adore) caught on a hand-line or fishing rod and not by trawling, when nets are involved. This is usually the way kingklip and hake are caught, which is why they should not be included in the linefish line-up.

When it comes to fish, the all-important question is 'Is it fresh?' In case you ever wondered, the word means recently off to fishy heaven – never frozen. Put another way, the terms 'fresh' and 'frozen' are mutually exclusive.

Want an honest answer from your favourite fishmonger? Ask 'How fresh is it?' rather than 'Is it fresh?' Check for signs of panic in his eyes when he replies, and be suspicious of terms like 'freshly frozen' which are designed to con you into supping on a creature far too long out of its watery habitat.

Let him know in no uncertain terms that you'd sooner arm-wrestle an octopus than accept sub-standard fish. The freshest often lurks behind the scenes in the cold-room. Despite this profound piece of economic insight, feel no pain about sending him scurrying into the bowels of his establishment to find the best.

Be sure to check it out properly before parting with your hard-earned cash. By the creature's colour and eyes (bright) and texture (firm), it's the easiest thing in the world to tell the difference between the good, the bad and the best left behind. If you're still uncertain, take a whiff. All lingering doubts will be instantly dispelled.

smoked trout frikkadels
with charred limes

Forget about plain fishcakes. Use smoked trout, give them an Indian zing with masala and fresh coriander, and call them frikkadels. If you can't find trout, any sort of fish will do, leftover or freshly cooked for the occasion. Serve frikkadels hot or at room temperature but never chilled, as they lose all their flavour.

makes about 12; serves 4 to 6

500g smoked trout fillets
sea salt and milled black pepper
300g potatoes, peeled and diced
60ml (4 tablespoons) finely chopped onion
45ml (3 tablespoons) chopped flat-leaf parsley
5ml (1 teaspoon) turmeric (borrie)
2 eggs, lightly beaten
small bunch coriander, chopped
5ml (1 teaspoon) roasted masala (page 24)
freshly squeezed juice of 1 lemon or lime
vegetable oil
charred limes, to serve (see posh tip)

tartare sauce
250ml (1 cup) mayonnaise (page 102)
1 hard-boiled egg, finely chopped
10ml (2 teaspoons) dijon mustard
15ml (1 tablespoon) drained capers

Skin and flake the trout, jettisoning all the bones. Place in a large bowl and season generously with salt and pepper.

Cook the potato in salted boiling water. Drain well. Mash and season with salt and pepper. Mix in the fish, onion, parsley, turmeric, egg, coriander and roasted masala, and flavour with lemon or lime juice. Form into patties, and flatten slightly between your palms.

tartare sauce Mix the ingredients together in a small bowl.

to serve Fry the frikkadels in hot oil until crisp and well browned. Drain on paper towel. Serve with tartare sauce and charred limes for squeezing.

makeahead
Frikkadels should be fried just before serving, but the mixture may be refrigerated for a day. Charred limes and tartare sauce are fine for an hour or two.

poshtip
Charred limes are fabulous with seafood. Cut a couple of limes in half, brush generously with olive oil and grill in a heavy frying pan until lightly charred and wonderfully smoky.

poshquaffing
The compendium of flavours in this medley directs vinous fare with attitude. Blanc fumé (oaked sauvignon blanc) delivers. The grassy fruit spikes the smoky, oil-rich trout, counters the masala, and its wood vanillins spar with the charred limes. Steely riesling blends initially support the plate but flag, and reds turn metallic.

'Frikkadels' is a lovely old-fashioned word I grew up with. It refers both to fishcakes and meatballs. My mom would make big, fat ones for family dinners, and teeny ones to serve with drinks when friends came around. She would spear them on toothpicks and I always thought they looked extremely smart!

chilli-zapped fish
with an eastern twist

This seductive fish dish with an oriental attitude has shredded vegetables to add colour and crunch. Any fresh fish may be used, including red steenbras, stumpnose, geelbek, kob and dageraad. Even ordinary old hake, if there aren't any more exotic types on offer. Serve hot from the oven or cooled to room temperature.

serves 4

2 whole, fresh fish fillets, trimmed and skinned (about 800g in total)
sea salt and milled black pepper
30ml (2 tablespoons) medium dry sherry
30ml (2 tablespoons) soy sauce
15ml (1 tablespoon) ketjap manis (sweet soy sauce)
5ml (1 teaspoon) sesame oil
1 red or green chilli, seeded and very finely sliced
2 garlic cloves, peeled and finely chopped
4 thin slices fresh ginger, finely shredded
250g vegetables cut into fine threads (red or yellow pepper,
   mangetout, celery, courgettes)

Lay the fish fillets in a dish to fit snugly and season lightly with salt and pepper. Mix together the sherry, soy sauce, ketjap manis, sesame oil, chilli, garlic and ginger in a small jug, and pour over the fish. Cover and set aside in a cool spot for an hour to marinate, or refrigerate for a couple of hours if you prefer.

Heat the oven to 180ºC. Scatter the vegetables into a casserole; choose one large enough to accommodate the fish in one layer. Lift the fish from the marinade and place on top of the vegetables. Pour the marinade over, cover with foil and bake for 25 to 30 minutes until the fish is done, and the flesh is opaque right through.

to serve Lift the fish fillets from the baking dish and place on a serving platter. Top with the cooked vegetables and pour over the baking liquid.

makeahead

Let the marinating time dictate your timing schedule. It's surprisingly flexible, and the fish can be set aside to gain flavour for anything from 30 minutes to three hours.

poshquaffing

'Drink what you cook with' is an old kitchen adage, and sherry promises to meet and match the oriental charm that oozes from this dish. It doesn't hold up, however, and the individual character of the sauce wins through. Support it, and your palate, with draughts of chilled, dry white. Entry-level blends, often sauvignon-based, refresh.

soy sauce, a must-have pantry item, is made from naturally fermented soy beans, wheat or barley flour and water. The flavour is gloriously rich and slightly salty, so take care when adding extra salt. You'll find light soy sauce (thin and better for cooking) and dark soy sauce (thicker and sweeter; good as a dipping sauce). Ketjap manis is even sweeter and gloriously sticky, while teriyaki sauce is a mixture of soy sauce, sugar, ginger and spices.

Choose your fish with care; a life-time of catching, cooking and feasting on the freshest of Neptune's bounty has taught me that less than perfect seafood should be given the short shrift it deserves.

barbecued linefish
with tomato, pawpaw and caper salsa

Use any linefish you fancy, but the cooking method (barbecuing or grilling) is simple, so fresh fish is infinitely preferable to frozen. My favourites for this recipe include red or white steenbras, geelbek and kob. Even gamefish like yellowtail and tuna would be good. Have fun with the salsa: add shredded chilli or loads of chopped flat-leaf parsley; use avocado or sweet melon instead of pawpaw; replace the coriander with rocket.

serves 4

4 fillets fresh linefish (skin on), each about 200g
sea salt and milled black pepper
6 bay leaves, lightly crushed
60ml (4 tablespoons) olive oil
freshly squeezed juice of 1 lemon or lime
4 garlic cloves, peeled and crushed

tomato, pawpaw and caper salsa
200g cocktail tomatoes, quartered
1 small pawpaw, skinned and cut into small cubes
small bunch coriander, chopped
45ml (3 tablespoons) drained capers
45ml (3 tablespoons) olive oil
freshly squeezed juice of 2 limes or 1 large lemon

Place the fish fillets in a dish to fit snugly, and season with salt and pepper. Scatter over the bay leaves. Mix together the olive oil, lemon or lime juice and garlic, and pour over. Cover and refrigerate for 3 to 4 hours to marinate. Turn the fish occasionally so that it flavours evenly.

tomato, pawpaw and caper salsa Mix the tomatoes, pawpaw, coriander and capers together in a bowl. Drizzle over the olive oil and flavour the salsa with lime or lemon juice, salt and pepper. Toss everything together gently.

Just before serving, lift the fish from the marinade and barbecue skin-down over medium-hot coals until gloriously browned. Then turn and cook skin-down until done. If grilling the fish, place on a foil-lined tray. Grill close to a hot oven grill until done right through – this will take 7 to 10 minutes, depending upon the thickness and texture of the fish. There's no need to turn it while cooking. Take care you don't overcook the fish and dry it out. Test for doneness by parting the flesh with two forks and taking a peek; it should be opaque right through.

to serve Place the fish on warm plates and spoon a little salsa on top or alongside.

makeahead
The marinade is so gentle that the fish won't mind languishing in it for up to eight hours in the fridge. Salsa will be fine in the fridge for about four hours; longer than that and it gets limp and soggy.

poshtip
Linefish refers to pelagic fish living in the open sea, usually near the surface, which are caught on a line (hand-line or fishing rod) and not by other methods, such as trawling, when nets are involved.

poshquaffing
Despite headline status, fish is not this plate's signal flavour – that comes from the electric salsa. No matter, as the best culinary match is with sauvignon blanc: it partners the heady accompaniment as well as it does the linefish. Sauvignon blends with chardonnay add a little extra, the latter being comfortably at home with capers.

poached fish
on mushroom risotto

This dashing dish is crammed with flavour and perfect for any fresh fish that you may find at your fishmonger.

serves 6

4 portions filleted, skinless fresh fish, each about 200g
sea salt and milled black pepper
750ml (3 cups) fish stock or chicken stock (page 15)
125ml (½ cup) dry white wine
2 leeks, trimmed and finely sliced
15ml (1 tablespoon) black or white peppercorns
small bunch marjoram or oregano

mushroom risotto
50g butter
400g white button or portabellini mushrooms, wiped and sliced
250g risotto rice
1 litre (4 cups) hot stock (from poaching the fish)

Place the fish in a saucepan large enough to accommodate the fillets in a single layer. Season generously with salt and pepper. Bring the stock to the boil in a saucepan with the wine, leeks, peppercorns and marjoram or oregano. Cover and simmer gently for about 15 minutes for the flavours to infuse.

Strain sufficient stock over the fish to cover it completely, and simmer for 5 to 7 minutes until just cooked through; cooking time depends on thickness and density of the flesh (part the flesh to check if it's opaque right through).

Lift the fish onto a plate, cover with foil and keep warm. Strain the stock for the risotto.

mushroom risotto Heat the butter in a medium saucepan, add the mushrooms and cook gently until they soften, stirring constantly. Season with salt and pepper. Tip in the rice and stir until the grains are well coated in the buttery pan juices.

Add a ladleful of the stock and stir with a wooden spoon, loosening the rice from the sides and bottom of the pan. When the stock has been absorbed, add more. Continue in this way, stirring regularly but not obsessively. The rice is done when it's cooked through but still firm to the bite.

to serve Present the poached fish and mushroom risotto on separate plates or, for individual platings, spoon risotto onto hot plates and top with fish.

makeahead
Fish objects to standing around after being cooked, so pre-preparing it is a no-no. Have everything ready to go and do the cooking at the last minute. Purists wouldn't dream of making risotto in advance, either.

poshtip
If you haven't the time or patience to make your own fish stock, instant chicken stock will do, but make it very weak to avoid the flavour dominating the dish.

poshquaffing
Your optimum choice needs to match the dominant mushroom, contain the creamy texture of the risotto, and still not obscure the delicacy of the fish. Pinot noir does all of these, in either organic farmland or fresh cherry-fruit genres. If you can't manage red wine with fish, bold is best amongst the whites. Wooded chardonnay will stay the pace.

gamefish steaks
with a soufflé topping

This was a signature dish at Chardonnay, a restaurant I owned in Hout Bay in the mid-80s with my sister-in-law, Anne Klarie. She had winkled the recipe out of a chef in Hawaii. I adore making it to impress special friends when there's fresh yellowtail or angelfish to be had. Serve in individual baking dishes that retain the cooking liquid round each portion of fish. Alternatively, bake all four servings together in a dish that holds the pieces snugly and fits perfectly under the oven grill.

serves 4

mayonnaise
2 whole eggs
1 egg yolk
10ml (2 teaspoons) dijon mustard
sea salt and milled black pepper
30ml (2 tablespoons) white wine or cider vinegar
375ml (1½ cups) olive or vegetable oil (or mix the two)

4 fresh yellowtail or angelfish steaks, each about 200g and about 2cm thick
sea salt and milled black pepper
200ml (¾ cup) medium dry sherry
2 garlic cloves, peeled and crushed
4 spring onions, trimmed and finely sliced
paprika

mayonnaise In a food processor or blender, or with an electric mixer, whisk the eggs, egg yolk, mustard, and a little salt and pepper until pale and thick. With the machine running, add the vinegar, then the oil, pouring it in a thin, thin stream.

Skin the fish and season lightly with salt and pepper. Choose a frying pan just large enough to to accommodate all four pieces, add the sherry and garlic and bring to the boil. Add the fish, cover and poach over medium heat for 2 minutes, turning the fish once.

Check if the fish is done by gently parting the flesh to see if it's opaque. If not, simmer for another minute. Don't overcook the fish; if it dries out it will be tasteless and boring.

Heat the oven grill. Transfer the fish to individual baking dishes or one large dish, and pour a few tablespoons of poaching liquid over each portion. Top each with half a cupful of mayonnaise, smoothing it down the sides to cover the fish. Top with sliced spring onion, dust with paprika and grill for a few minutes until the topping is puffed and golden.

to serve Place individual serving dishes onto larger plates, or lift each portion onto warm plates and spoon around a little of the cooking liquid.

makeahead

This dish only takes a few minutes to make, so it's unwise to prepare it ahead. Have everything ready to go – fish portioned and skinned, mayonnaise made and sherry and garlic in the pan – before your guests arrive.

poshtips

Yellowtail and angelfish are preferred for their firm texture and distinctive flavour. The sherry must be medium dry. If you have none on hand, mix together dry and semi-sweet sherry. Most importantly, there's no substitute for home-made mayonnaise for the topping.

poshquaffing

Such opulence demands a contrast. The gamey fish and mayonnaise fold together in a cresdendo of riches, well ordered and elevated by sauvignon blanc. Select a tropical style though, as flinty grassiness can jar. ABS ('anything-but-sauvignon') club members may wish to try quieter exotica like pinot blanc, sylvaner or pinot gris.

Cooking is like magic: turning a few basic ingredients into something else entirely!

charred tuna
with spuds, tomatoes and green beans

This cheery, taste-bud zapping dish is one of the most drop-dead gorgeous creations of the French kitchen, where it is often served on a large platter for everyone to help themselves. It's excellent as a starter or main dish, and a great choice for times when fresh tuna is readily available.

serves 4

4 fresh tuna steaks, each about 100g
olive oil
sea salt and milled black pepper
12 new potatoes
150g slim green beans
1 red onion, finely sliced
4 anchovy fillets, drained and finely sliced
200g cocktail tomatoes or small roma tomatoes
24 calamata olives
mustard seed dressing (half the recipe; page 21)
small bunch flat-leaf parsley, chopped, for garnishing

Brush the tuna generously with olive oil and season with salt and pepper. Boil the potatoes in their jackets until soft. Cut in half or quarters, depending on size. Blanch the beans in salted boiling water until tender but not too floppy, then refresh in cold water. Drain well.

Heat a generous amount of olive oil in a medium frying pan and fry the onion until translucent. Add the anchovy and potatoes, and fry until golden. Add the beans, tomatoes and olives and heat through. Season with salt and pepper. Remove from the heat, pour over the mustard seed dressing, and mix in gently.

Heat a ridged grill-pan or heavy frying pan, add the tuna and char well on both sides. Don't cook it all the way through; the fish should be still rare in the centre.

to serve The simplest way is to plonk the tuna on top of the vegetables in the pan. Garnish with copious amounts of chopped parsley for old time's sake.

makeahead

Both the vegetables and the tuna may be served warm or at room temperature, so don't fret if they have to stand around for an hour or so before serving.

poshtip

If you're not mad about tuna, top the vegetables with sliced fillet steak that has been roasted whole over the coals.

poshquaffing

Relative newcomers like viognier, verdelho and grenache blanc are slowly jazzing up stalwarts sauvignon, chardonnay and semillon in dry white blends as plantings come on stream. They add exotic interest, just right for this flavoursome composition. Chardonnay suffices for the more conservative; lesser offerings are blown off the table.

This is one of those fuss-free recipes that may be served straight from the pan it's been cooked in.

seared fish
with caramelized chicory

Linefish and gamefish are plentiful in summer, so this is the best time to conjure up this seductive dish as you know the fish will be fresh. Flavourful tuna and marlin are perfect, but firm linefish like snoek, yellowtail and angelfish are also delicious. There's a growing move towards cooking gamefish medium-rare rather than all the way through. The choice I leave to you!

serves 4

caramelized chicory
500g small heads chicory (4–5)
30g (2 tablespoons) butter
15ml (1 tablespoon) brown sugar
125ml (½ cup) water
30ml (2 tablespoons) balsamic vinegar

4 fresh linefish or gamefish steaks (skin on), each about 200g
olive oil
sea salt and milled black pepper
spicy mashed potato, to serve (page 153)

caramelized chicory Trim the stalks, but leave the chicory whole. Melt the butter and brown sugar over gentle heat in a frying pan. Add the water, balsamic vinegar and chicory, and season with salt and pepper. Cook, turning regularly, until the chicory is tender and caramelized. They'll fall apart a bit, but that's part of the charm.

Heat a ridged grill-pan or heavy frying pan. Brush the fish liberally with olive oil and sear on both sides; press with a spatula so that it's well marked. Cook to the desired degree at a more gentle pace. Season with salt and pepper. If preferred, barbecue the fish as described on page 98

to serve Spoon spicy mashed potato onto warm plates. Top with fish and spoon caramelized chicory on the side.

makeahead
Caramelized chicory may be prepared several hours ahead. Reheat it and cook the fish just before serving.

posh**quaffing**
Versatile chenin blanc, industry workhorse, is great with chicory. Braised and caramelized with balsamic, it provides a bed for full-flavoured fish, and playmates for its wine partner. Seek a ripe, fruity version of chenin, with enough body to match the fish.

chicory, white-tipped, tightly packed, and pale yellow-green has crunchy, slightly bitter leaves. It's also known as endive (from the French) and witlof (from the Belgians who first produced it). While related to the lettuces, it belongs to the daisy family and its cousins include radicchio and escarole. Check that the outer leaves are bright and crisp; older specimens wilt and turn brown. Store chicory in a brown paper bag in the fridge.

I devised this marvellous mélange when we returned from a deep-sea
fishing trip off Cape Point with a catch of yellowtail and tuna aboard.
A quick raid of the fridge for stuff to serve it with, and even Neptune
would have been impressed; the fish didn't die in vain!

garlic and lemon prawns
flamed in whisky

Prawns, garlic, lemon and butter are soulmates, so I really don't see the point of reinventing the relationship and fixing something that ain't broke. As a nod to the posh theme of this book, though, they're flamed with whisky at the end, which adds oodles of flavour and more than a dash of drama if your guests are ogling the action.

serves 2 as a main course; 4 as a starter

10–12 large prawns (shells and heads on)
30ml (2 tablespoons) vegetable oil
100g butter
6–8 garlic cloves, peeled and crushed
125ml (½ cup) whisky
freshly squeezed lemon juice
sea salt and milled black pepper

Devein and rinse the prawns. Heat the oil and half the butter in a wide saucepan until sizzling hot. Stir in the garlic, then add the prawns and fry for about 30 seconds on each side. Warm the whisky (measure it into a metal soup ladle and heat over a flame), pour over and ignite. When the flames subside, cover the pan and reduce the heat to cook the prawns over very low heat for about 2 to 3 minutes, depending on size.

Remove from the heat, transfer the prawns to a warm plate and keep hot while quickly finishing off the sauce.

Cut the remaining butter into small pieces and, working off the heat, whisk vigorously into the pan juices. The sauce will thicken to a luscious, creamy consistency. If it gets too cool, place the pan on the heat for a few moments, then continue incorporating the butter as before. Flavour with a good squeeze of lemon juice and a little salt and pepper.

to serve Pour the sauce over the prawns and serve immediately with rice or crusty bread to mop up the glorious juices.

makeahead

Prawns are awful if they've been cooked too long before serving, so do your pre-prep ahead of time (prawns ready for the pan; butter and oil at hand; garlic peeled) and dart into the kitchen at the very last moment.

poshquaffing

Even without the posh tizzy of being flamed in whisky, this is chardonnay territory. A full-frontal bottling, replete with zesty lime and smoky oak, is required to temper the shellfish and host the garlic and lemon. Then again, why not try a single malt whisky softened with spring water...?

prawns, shrimps and langoustines are all delicious in this recipe, even though they differ in appearance, texture and size. Cut the shell down the back with scissors and pull out the alimentary canal (vein). Langoustines or large prawns may be cut right through which makes them even easier to clean. If you prefer, remove and discard the head too.

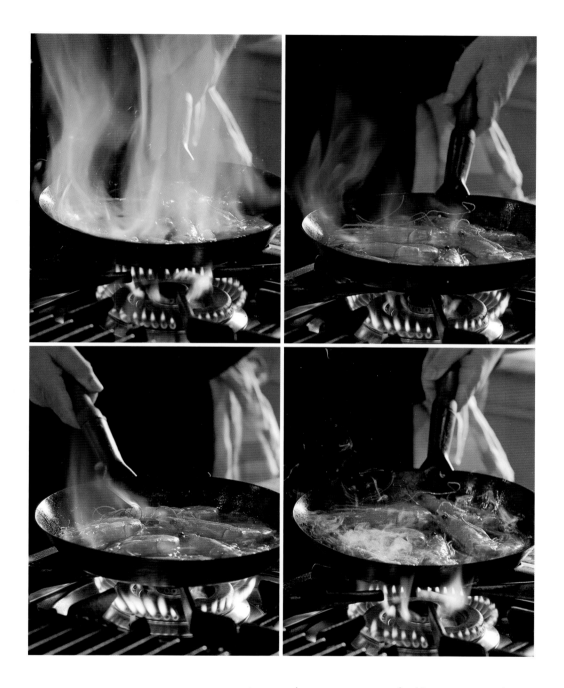

Munching prawn shells and sucking
all the flavour from their legs is one of the best treats in the
world, so don't even think of using shelled prawns in this recipe.

char-grilled crayfish
with roasted tomatoes and peppers

An extrovert dish with a riot of colour and taste. And wonderfully sociable, thanks to the dressing in which to dunk your crayfish if you feel like eating with your fingers. Crusty peasant bread on the side is a good idea. Grilled crayfish has a powerful flavour and enjoys a flavour-zapped accompaniment such as these roasted tomatoes and peppers.

serves 4

4–8 crayfish tails (depending on size)
olive oil
sea salt and milled black pepper
roasted tomatoes and peppers, to serve (page 151)

basil and chilli dressing
10 large basil leaves
1 chilli, sliced in half and seeded
2 garlic cloves, peeled
60ml (4 tablespoons) olive oil
freshly squeezed juice of 1 lime
50g butter, cut into small chunks

Cut the crayfish shells through the back, so they hinge at the belly. Devein, rinse well and pat dry. Place flesh-up in a flat dish, drizzle liberally with olive oil and season with salt and pepper.

basil and chilli dressing Pound together the basil leaves, chilli, garlic, olive oil and lime juice in a pestle and mortar or with a food processor. Pour over the crayfish and place in the fridge to marinate. The time depends entirely on your schedule; anything from 30 minutes to several hours will be fine.

Drain the crayfish and scrape the dressing into a medium saucepan. Bring to the boil and finish the sauce off by whisking in the butter bit by bit. Season with salt and pepper.

Meanwhile, heat a ridged grill-pan and char the crayfish until it's cooked, turning occasionally and brushing with olive oil from time to time. This will take between 6 and 8 minutes, depending on the size of the tails. Better still, barbecue the crayfish on a grid over medium-hot coals.

to serve Arrange the crayfish on warm plates. Drizzle over the hot dressing and spoon roasted tomatoes and peppers alongside.

makeahead
Once the crayfish is marinating in the fridge, the hard part is over. All you need to do is cook them and finish the sauce. Roasted tomatoes and peppers are happily served hot from the oven or cooled to room temperature, so they aren't a problem either.

poshtip
Crayfish tails freeze more successfully than the whole creature, so don't hesitate to use them in this recipe if you can't lay your hands on fresh ones.

poshquaffing
No, not even full-frontal chardonnay is enough here. The power of grilled crayfish, an emphatic marinade and dressing and singular sides call for a little more. Semillon, underrated and unfashionable, brings complex candle-wax breadth to 'The Big C' in a blend. Although you'll seldom find the S' word on a dry white blend label, grill your retailer.

Crayfish (officially called rock lobsters) are a sought-after form of edible underwater life despite the price and the fact that they're visually challenged (not in your wildest dreams would you call them pretty).

Then again, some of our most inspired edibles come in forms that probably terrified those intrepid forebears who first shut their eyes, cooked them, loved them and changed the course of culinary history forever.

When we were small our dad farmed chickens, and my sisters and I spent many happy hours watching as they scratched about in their roomy 'fowl hoks' pecking for the choicest bits. As farm kids tend to do, we learned early on to avoid having a personal relationship with any of our feathered friends, so were quite brave about taking ringside seats during the slaughtering process, convincing ourselves that the chooks died young but happy (and for a good cause).

For Sunday lunch we invariably tucked into succulent roast chicken, crisp skin basted with a mixture of butter, the bird's own fat and a little lemon juice, salt and pepper. All the trimmings accompanied this most excellent of feasts: potatoes and onions roasted alongside the bird, cauliflower cheese, glazed carrots and lashings of gravy made from the pan juices. No wonder this spectacular meal is still my favourite, bar none!

The chickens of my childhood would today be referred to as organic, free-range birds, and these are the ones to buy if you have the choice. When it comes to flavour and texture, there is simply no comparison with birds intensively farmed and reared in batteries (poor creatures), and the extra cost is well worthwhile. Besides the sumptuous flesh, you'll have a sturdy carcass for stock, if you have the patience for this most satisfying of tasks. The recipe is on page 15.

Besides the farming method, age matters; younger, smaller birds are more delicate, while larger, older fowls are more flavourful, perfectly suited to robust cooking methods such as pot-roasting long and slow.

Consider your recipe when deciding whether to purchase whole, portioned or filleted chicken. A whole bird may be cheaper per kilogram, but nearly half is bone, so ready-to-cook portions that have little wastage may be your best bet.

Besides the cost factor, there's also a time saving in the preparation: cutting up a chicken takes longer than simply opening the pack of breasts, thighs or drumsticks.

Chicken is perfect for a wide range of cooking methods – roasting, pot-roasting, baking, frying, grilling and barbecuing. And, while the simplest recipes are often the best, chicken thoroughly enjoys being flavoured with a wide range of herbs and spices, not to mention a variety of vegetables – especially if it's a pale, characterless, mass-farmed specimen. With a little ingenuity, each chicken dish you prepare can break new grounds in the flavour stakes.

chicken on curried pulses
with beetroot crisps

Chicken is perfect with our fabulous medley of gently curried lentils and chickpeas. Give wings to your imagination when preparing it, adding goodies like green peas, whole kernel corn and cannellini beans to plump it out for unexpected guests. Crisp beetroot is a snappy surprise.

serves 4

4 free-range chicken breasts on the bone
250ml (1 cup) chicken stock (page 15)
soy, garlic and sesame dressing (page 21)
curried pulses (page 152)
60ml (¼ cup) sesame seeds, roasted in a dry frying pan

beetroot crisps
2 uncooked beetroot
vegetable oil

Skin and trim the chicken breasts. Bring the stock to the boil in a medium saucepan. Add the chicken, cover and poach over medium heat for 15 to 20 minutes until cooked through. Cool the chicken in the stock.

Bone the chicken, cut into thickish slices and place in a dish. Pour over the soy, garlic and sesame dressing and set aside for about an hour to marinate. Prepare the curried pulses.

beetroot crisps Peel and slice the beetroot very finely with a potato peeler. Deep fry in hot oil for 2 to 3 minutes. When they change colour, they're done. Drain on paper towels.

to serve Spoon the curried pulses on a large platter or individual plates. Drain the chicken, pile on top and moisten with a little of the dressing. Garnish with beetroot crisps and sesame seeds.

makeahead

Don't even think about chilling chicken after poaching. Curried pulses are far more forgiving, though, and may be covered and chilled for up to a day.

poshtip

If you don't feel like making your own beetroot crisps, garnish the dish with store-bought root vegetable chips.

poshquaffing

'Chicken' is in lights, but it's the curried pulses with which to contend: cumin, coriander and cardamom are challenging. Aromatic varieties, dry or off-dry, proffer scents to match and refreshing body as a foil. Floral riesling does best, unusual dry muscat d'Alexandrie is a surprise. Blanc de noir wines are easy alternatives with more flesh.

brown lentils, heroes of our curried pulses, are earthy, nutty, nutritious (and fashionable) and come in different varieties from red to pale green, slate grey and brown. When prepared with a little imagination, they're light years away from the boring hippie sixties staple. Puy lentils are my favourite. They have a peppery taste and keep their shape without turning to sludge. The cooking time of lentils varies according to their type and age. Test by munching a couple; they should be nice and tender.

fried chicken,
mashed peas and corn cakes

There's something wonderfully comforting about chicken, peas and corn, a tasty threesome that reminds me of childhood meals. Here they're glammed up a tad for more discerning audiences, without losing any of their homely charm.

serves 6

6 filleted, skinless free-range chicken breasts
sea salt and milled black pepper
60ml (4 tablespoons) olive oil
30ml (2 tablespoons) soy sauce
corn cakes (page 151)
lemon or lime wedges, for sqeezing

mashed peas
500ml (2 cups) fresh or frozen green peas
butter
8 spring onions, trimmed and very finely sliced
60ml (4 tablespoons) verjuice or dry white wine
125ml (½ cup) cream

Place the chicken in a shallow dish and season lightly with salt and pepper. Pour over the olive oil and soy sauce and turn to coat all over. Set aside in a cool spot for an hour or two.

mashed peas Defrost the peas if they're frozen. Melt a good knob of butter in a medium saucepan, add the peas and spring onion and stir-fry for a minute or two. Add the verjuice or wine and cream, and season with salt and pepper. Simmer uncovered for 2 to 3 minutes until the peas are soft. Take care they don't lose their bright colour. Whiz everything in a food processor until smooth. Return to a clean saucepan and reheat just before serving.

Heat a ridged grill-pan until piping hot. Drain the chicken beasts and grill until well marked. Reduce the heat and cook through at a more gentle pace. Fry the corn cakes at the same time.

to serve Place corn cakes on warm plates and top with mashed peas, with a chicken breast perched nattily on top, and a couple of lemon or lime wedges for squeezing.

verjuice, verjus or *vert jus* (green juice), is the unfermented juice of unripe grapes. Use freely in cooking to replace lemon juice and vinegar, even to deglaze the pan after frying or roasting. It adds body and flavour as it reduces, and thickens up when a touch of cream or bits of butter are whisked in, for example, when preparing a beurre blanc. Verjuice should be refrigerated after opening and it will last for a couple of months.

makeahead
You're welcome to get the chicken ready a day ahead; it won't mind languishing in the fridge in the marinade. Mashed peas may also be chilled for a day but over-cooking will dull the colour, so reheat with care. Corn cakes are best straight from the pan.

poshquaffing
Disarmingly rich, this dish requires a dry white of substance, yet one without loud individuality. Sauvignon blanc in restrained rather than opulent herbaceous style is our choice. Lightly wooded chardonnay will also do, but risks enhancing the inherent creaminess. A crisp blend of the two covers all bases.

When planning the menu, it makes sense to consider the preferences
of your guests. But always please yourself as well.

pan-roasted chicken
with herb-crushed spuds

There's a robust feel about this uncomplicated chicken dish that has its heart deep in the Italian countryside where we holidayed in an old farmhouse and prepared it from ingredients from the local market. Chicken thighs work best, as they're the most succulent part of the chicken and are very forgiving in terms of cooking time. You could, however, use drumsticks or a whole chicken, jointed and skinned.

serves 4 to 5

8 free-range chicken thighs
olive oil
sea salt and milled black pepper
125ml (½ cup) dry white wine
30ml (2 tablespoons) lemon juice
3–4 thin strips lemon peel (use a vegetable peeler)
5 garlic cloves, peeled and roughly chopped
2 sprigs rosemary, snipped into small pieces
30ml (2 tablespoons) chopped fennel
2 large, ripe tomatoes, blanched, skinned and quartered (see page 63)
herb-crushed spuds, to serve (page 153)

Skin the chicken and trim off all visible fat. Heat a little olive oil in a large saucepan with a well-fitting lid. The chicken pieces should fit snugly without overlapping. Lightly brown the chicken all over, working over medium-high heat; watch carefully and turn the portions frequently so they don't stick to the pan. Season with salt and pepper.

Warm the wine and lemon juice in a small saucepan with the lemon peel, garlic, rosemary and fennel. Pour over the chicken, add the tomatoes and cover. Cook over very low heat until the chicken is done (about 40 minutes), turning the pieces occasionally.

to serve Transfer the chicken and tomatoes to a warm serving platter, cover with foil and keep warm. Boil the pan juices uncovered, stirring occasionally, until reduced and nicely thickened. Strain over the chicken and serve piping hot with herb-crushed spuds.

makeahead

Prepare the dish up to a day ahead prior to removing the chicken from the pan and reducing the pan juices. Cover and refrigerate. Warm up shortly before serving. Herb-crushed potatoes don't mind being reheated, so make ahead and set aside for a couple of hours while you get on with other things. They aren't so great next day, though, as the herbs lose their fresh flavour and bright colour.

poshtip

Glam this dish up even more with pitted or stuffed green olives. Add to the pan about 10 minutes before the chicken is done.

poshquaffing

Sauvignon blanc brings a herby ring to the verdant frame and lifts the potatoes' pith. Fleshy chenin blanc enhances the sumptuous texture. Both are 'safe'. Posh is not about safety though, so experiment with fernão pires or even lighter-styled (in local climes) Italian reds like sangiovese, nebbiolo, barbera...

flat-roast chicken
with caramelized vegetables

This one-dish chicken and vegetable creation cooks unattended to crisp perfection and may be served directly from the roaster. Use any vegetables your heart desires: potato wedges, whole baby beetroot, fennel bulbs, tiny onions, sliced peppers, courgettes and parsnips are all delicious done this way.

serves 4

1 bunch thyme
1 whole free-range chicken
4 baby butternut, trimmed and cut in half
2 turnips, scrubbed and cut into quarters
4–6 small, whole carrots, scrubbed
peeled cloves from 1 head garlic
2 limes, cut in half
olive oil and butter
sea salt and milled black pepper

Heat the oven to 200ºC. Lightly oil a large roaster and place the bunch of thyme in the centre.

Cut off and discard the backbone of the chicken and press hard on the breastbone so the bird lies flat. Rinse clean and place, skin up, on the thyme. Surround with the vegetables and garlic cloves. Squeeze over the lime juice, splosh liberally with olive oil, dot with butter and season generously with salt and pepper.

Roast uncovered for about 50 minutes until the chicken is done (thigh-juices run clear when pierced with a skewer) and the vegetables have caramelized in the pan juices.

to serve Lift the chicken and vegetables onto a warm platter and serve piping hot. If you think the meal needs a little extra something, offer a simple green salad dressed with thyme and walnut oil dressing (page 21).

makeahead

Although this dish needs no attention while it cooks, serve it straight from the oven; chicken skin becomes wrinkled and ugly if it languishes about. Rather assemble the dish in the roaster a couple of hours ahead, and pop it into the oven about an hour before serving. Refrigerate between preparation and roasting.

poshquaffing

Chicken is magnanimous with wine. Its broad texture, the unimposing root vegetables and warmth of thyme call for mouth-filling, comfort quaffing. Chenin blanc, equally generous with chicken in its various forms, supports the flesh, copes with the caramelized coating and elevates the veggies.

thyme, an outspoken herb, is a culinary charmer and medicinal marvel. My herb patch is edged with rows of it, and I love the lemony, spicy smell that rises as I brush past. In olden times ladies in crinolines planted 'thyme walks' in their gardens for the same reason. A more modern twist is to plant thyme near your outdoor spa bath; the warmth of the steam has a similar effect. Thyme leaves are so tiny that there's no need to chop them before cooking; simply strip from the stems with your fingers from tip to base.

After bringing this dish into the oven, the magic happens independently of what you do, so there's no need to stay in the kitchen and miss out on the gossip.

comorian coconut chicken
with gremolata

Coconut chicken (gently simmered in coconut cream flavoured with that fabulous foursome of garlic, ginger, turmeric and chilli) is my favourite dish from the laid-back Indian Ocean islands of the Comores. The islanders joint a whole chicken and use the milk of fresh coconuts; ready-skinned thighs and coconut cream from a tin are easier options. The twist in this recipe is the gremolata garnish. Purists may object (it's not faithful to the original dish) but delish nevertheless.

serves 4

8 free-range chicken thighs
sea salt and milled black pepper
cake flour
vegetable oil
2 onions, finely chopped
6 garlic cloves, peeled and finely chopped
3cm piece fresh ginger, scraped and grated
2ml (½ teaspoon) turmeric (borrie)
1 red or green chilli, sliced and seeded
leaves stripped from a small bunch thyme
60ml (4 tablespoons) tomato purée
400ml tin coconut cream

gremolata
finely grated zest of 1 lemon
small bunch flat-leaf parsley, chopped
6 garlic cloves, peeled and very finely chopped

Skin the chicken, season with salt and pepper and dust with a little flour. Brown lightly all over in oil in a deep saucepan. Remove from the pan and set aside.

Add the onion to the pan (with a little extra oil if necessary) and fry until golden. Add the garlic, ginger, turmeric, chilli and thyme. Return the chicken to the pan, pour over the tomato purée and coconut cream, cover and simmer over very gentle heat for about 30 minutes until cooked.

gremolata Mix the ingredients together in a small bowl.

to serve Lift the chicken onto a warm serving dish. If necessary, boil the sauce uncovered to thicken it a little, then pour over chicken. Serve with rice and gremolata to scatter on top.

makeahead
Comorian coconut chicken is even better next day, so prepare it ahead and reheat gently on the stove-top or in a low oven. Don't take liberties with gremolata, though; it should be freshly prepared.

poshtip
Take care with the quality of the tomato purée you use; peel and crush fresh, ripe tomatoes or use one of the excellent bottled purées about that are sweet and gentle. At all costs, avoid the harsh tinned stuff.

poshquaffing
The 'fabulous foursome' deserves the 'trendy threesome' – VVS. Short for viognier/verdelho/sauvignon blanc, and harbinger of a wave of white blends built around viognier, the new cult variety. Its sexy, peach-pip/apricot ring is perfect for the spice, coconut cream, lemon, parsley ... indeed everything in this lusty island special.

Gremolata — a fresh and free-spirited mix of chopped parsley, grated lemon peel and crushed garlic — is the traditional topping of osso bucco, but its fame has spread. The charm lies in the fact that it's lively mouth-feel is such an unexpected treat.

pot-roast chicken
with garlic, herbs and fennel

Pot-roasting keeps in all the moisture while nudging every drop of flavour from the chicken, which then mingles magically with the flavours you're adding to the pot, forming an utterly delicious gravy.

serves 4 to 5

1 free-range chicken
sea salt and milled black pepper
2 oranges
olive oil
1 onion, finely sliced
peeled cloves from 1 head garlic
1 bunch herbs (parsley, thyme, marjoram)
6 small fennel bulbs, trimmed
125ml (½ cup) dry white wine
125ml (½ cup) chicken stock (page 15)
10ml (2 teaspoons) dijon mustard
wine-glazed new potatoes, to serve (page 153)

Wash and dry the chicken and season inside and out with salt and pepper. Score one of the oranges with a knife to release the flavour and aroma, and stuff it into the body cavity. Cut the remaining orange into quarters.

Heat a little olive oil in a deep saucepan and brown the chicken lightly all over. Remove from the pan and set aside. Stir the onion and garlic into the pan juices and cook over high heat until lightly browned. Return the chicken to the pan and place the orange quarters, herbs and fennel around. Mix together the wine, stock and mustard, and pour over. Cover and cook very gently for about 90 minutes until the chicken is done.

to serve Lift the chicken and fennel onto a warm serving plate. Discard the orange pieces and herbs. Boil the sauce uncovered until reduced, thickened and absolutely delicious. Pour over the chicken and vegetables. Present wine-glazed new potatoes in a separate bowl.

makeahead

This dish cooks itself, so there's no need to pfaff around with it when you'd rather be regaling your guests with merry quip and jest. Simply decide when (about) you want to serve the main course and pop the chicken into the oven in good time.

poshtips

To prevent the liquid boiling away, use a pot with a well-fitting lid. Check from time to time, and add a little boiling water if needs be. For a better looking bird, pop the chicken into a very hot oven for a few minutes just before serving it. For a complete meal in one, add extra vegetables like baby carrots and peeled pickling onions to the pan about 20 minutes before the end of the cooking time.

poshquaffing

The roast is like a luxury train, vehicle for a kaleidoscope of flavours as it draws towards its final destination. Wine joins the fray to spotlight its fellow passengers: garlic and mixed herbs, orange infusion, liquorice-like fennel, wine glaze .... Judiciously wooded chardonnay is just right, even better if blended with voluptuous semillon.

fennel is closely related to the anise-flavoured herb, and the same feathery leaves can be seen emerging from its fat, overlapping stalks that form the plump, edible bulb. Trim away the stalks and string as you would celery, and halve or quarter the bulbs if they're large.

Next to my husband, my favourite man is my butcher – he has saved me from more culinary botches than I care to remember. When it comes to the need to know what you're doing, no other ingredient comes close to meat, so you need all the help you can get in this department!

In fact, several butchers cater to my meaty requirements: one especially for free-range pork, something I'm particularly fond of (pork and pork products from happy pigs that have spent time in the sun is infinitely more flavourful than that from their pale and uninteresting mass-farmed cousins) and for which I'm prepared to travel vast distances and spend a little extra of my hard-earned cash.

Pork enjoys hearty, basic cooking methods and doesn't do show-off elegance well. Think pot-roasted necks, barbecued chops, pan-fried loins, crisp, fatty belly strips and large roasts trapped in incredibly crusty crackling. My mother-in-law called it 'shrapnel', a rather apt description, not so? Here's how she made a perfect roast: score the rind of the joint if your butcher hasn't done so already. Pour plenty of boiling water over, place in a roaster and refrigerate for a couple of hours so the rind dries out. Rub the skin all over with vinegar and olive oil, and sprinkle liberally with sea salt. Roast at 220°C for 30 minutes, then reduce the heat to 160°C until the meat is done (calculate 25 minutes per 500g). Sprinkle the crackling lightly with flour and increase the oven temperature to 220°C for another 25 minutes or so until crisp.

Pork is a versatile meat, and good with a vast range of sidekicks such as root vegetables, white beans and olives. In terms of flavouring, pork adores garlic, a hint of anchovy, the juice and zest of citrus fruit, and mustard of all descriptions. As far as herbs are concerned, stay with sturdier types like rosemary, thyme, sage and lavender.

Pork and fruit marry well, but I think this is sometimes overdone, and much prefer the sweetness toned down a tad with lemon juice and vinegar, wine or verjuice. A little apple or redcurrant jelly melted into the gravy at the end – maybe a dash of marsala – is triumphant, adding a little sweetness and a nice gloss.

boozy pork fillets
with wine-plumped apricots

In summer, figs are wonderful in this dish. Cook as described for the apricots, or simply peel them and serve fresh. Another way is to cut them in half and roast briefly under a hot oven grill.

serves 4

wine-plumped apricots
250g soft-dried apricots
grated zest and juice of 1 lemon
125ml (½ cup) dry white wine
5ml (1 teaspoon) brown sugar
4 whole cloves
1 cinnamon stick

2–3 plump pork fillets (about 800g)
sea salt and milled black pepper
butter and olive oil
125ml (½ cup) chopped herbs (parsley, oregano, basil, tarragon, thyme)
125ml (½ cup) Galliano
125ml (½ cup) dry white wine

wine-plumped apricots Place the apricots in a small saucepan with the lemon zest and juice, wine, brown sugar, cloves and cinnamon. Top up with sufficient cold water to cover the fruit. Cover and simmer for about 3 minutes until soft. Uncover and cook briskly until the syrup has thickened slightly. Set aside to cool.

Trim the pork and season with salt and pepper. Heat a knob of butter and a little oil in a large frying pan until it starts to sizzle and brown. Toss in half the herbs, then add the pork and brown well all over, rubbing it into the pan to gain colour. Cover and cook over very low heat for about 12 minutes until the meat is done.

Pour over the Galliano and flame. When the flames die down, lift the meat from the pan and keep warm. Add the wine to the pan and simmer until the sauce thickens nicely, scraping up all the browning to make it rich and tasty. Stir in the remaining herbs.

to serve Arrange the pork on one large platter, or do individual servings. Pour over the sauce, garnish with wine-plumped apricots and serve immediately. Mashed potato rounds out the dish.

makeahead
Wine-plumped apricots are fine in the fridge for a day or two in a covered bowl. Pork must be served immediately it's cooked, but sizzling it up takes only a few minutes after all ingredients are readied, chopped and measured.

poshtip
Galliano is an Italian aniseed and liquorice liqueur. If you haven't any on hand, use medium sweet sherry or marsala.

poshquaffing
A dish as opulent as its name calls for a full, ripe – and equally tipsy – wine match. Modern show-stopping whites, oozing plump fruit, redolent of toasty oak and tingling with sturdy alcohol fit the bill magnificently. Chardonnay is obvious but a touch too buttery; honeyed semillon or tropical chenin blanc are more posh.

Pork is happiest when cooked with booze (white wine and Galliano are gorgeous together) and something sweet to cut through the richness – apricots in wine and spices are just the thing.

singaporean chilli pork

This tempting creation evolved from visits to the tiny island republic of Singapore which celebrates the cuisines of the island's peoples – Chinese, Indian and Malay, as well as Nonya, which is a merging of Chinese and Malay influences. As in all hot, humid climates, powerful flavours tempt heat-jaded appetites, so ingredients such as chilli, cardamom, cinnamon, cloves, lemon grass, tamarind, turmeric, garlic and ginger are woven into dishes to alluring effect.

serves 4

2–3 pork fillets, trimmed (about 800g)
sea salt and milled black pepper
vegetable oil
60ml (¼ cup) rice wine or medium dry sherry
1 onion, very finely sliced
4 garlic cloves, peeled and finely chopped
10ml (2 teaspoons) scraped and finely chopped fresh ginger
1 green chilli, finely sliced (leave seeds in for extra heat)
30ml (2 tablespoons) ketjap manis (sweet soy sauce)
125ml (½ cup) chicken stock (page 15)
200g dried egg noodles or rice noodles
coriander leaves, for garnishing

Trim the pork and slice diagonally into thick pieces, enlarging as you work towards the thinner ends to make them as even as possible. Whack with the flat side of a large knife to flatten them a little, and season with a little salt and pepper.

Heat a dash of oil in a frying pan and brown the meat well all over. Add the rice wine or sherry, cover and cook the meat for about 5 minutes – the centre should be slightly tinged with pink. Remove from the pan, set aside and keep hot.

Add the onion, garlic, ginger and chilli to the pan and fry gently until limp. Stir in the ketjap manis and stock, and boil briskly uncovered until the sauce thickens slightly. Return the meat to the pan and heat through.

Pour boiling water over the noodles in a bowl and set aside for about 2 minutes to soften. Drain well in a colander.

to serve Pile noodles into warm bowls and top with pork. Garnish with a little extra sliced chilli if you dare, and offer coriander separately, in case not everyone is fond of it.

makeahead

It's important to cook this dish just before serving, so get all the ingredients ready and dash into the kitchen at the last possible moment.

poshtips

If you don't have any ketjap manis on hand, substitute 30ml (2 tablespoons) soy sauce and 15ml (1 tablespoon) brown sugar. And if you're not crazy about chilli, simply leave it out.

poshquaffing

The creation of a hot climate, turboed with chilli, demands some 'coolth'. Chilled, bone-dry gewürztraminer cajoles the delicacy of the pork while keeping tongue-sting at arm's length, and freshens the palate for the next delectable fork-full. Fleshy pinot noir adds texture to the weave for hedonists; chardonnay is consigned to awkward adolescence.

Powerful oriental flavours and the zip of chilli in this dish will tempt the pickiest palate.

mustard-braised pork neck
with prunes

Here's a warming winter dish that is absolutely delicious, dead easy to make and cooked in one pot. It's a great recipe for easy entertaining, the pork slow-cooked with mustard, brown sugar and bags of whisky.

serves 8

1 whole boned, rolled pork neck (about 2 kg)
sea salt and milled black pepper
125ml (½ cup) brown sugar
125ml (½ cup) wholegrain mustard
butter and vegetable oil
200ml (¾ cup) whisky
500ml (2 cups) chicken stock (page 15)
60ml (4 tablespoons) chopped flat-leaf parsley
30ml (2 tablespoons) chopped sage
250g sun-dried prunes

If the pork hasn't been rolled in a net bag by your butcher, truss neatly with string. Season with salt and pepper. Mix together the brown sugar and mustard and smear over the meat.

Heat a generous amount of butter and oil in a heavy saucepan over medium heat and seal the meat all over. (Watch carefully; the coating burns if the heat is too high.)

Warm half the whisky, pour over the meat and flame. When the flames die down, add the stock, parsley and sage. Turn the meat in the sauce, cover and simmer very gently for 1½ to 2 hours, depending on the size of the pork neck. Turn the meat in the sauce from time to time so it flavours and cooks evenly. Add the prunes 10 minutes before the end of the cooking time.

to serve Lift the pork from the sauce, remove the net bag (string can remain on until you've carved the meat) and place on a warm platter with the prunes. Cover with foil and keep warm. Add the remaining whisky to the sauce and boil uncovered until it thickens slightly. Pour over the meat and garnish, if you wish, with fresh herbs.

makeahead

This is a perfect make-ahead dish. After plating it and napping with sauce, cover with foil and chill overnight in the fridge. Reheat gently (still covered) in a moderate oven.

poshquaffing

Simmered, sweet and sticky, the pork gains zest from mustard and a fillip from shards of spirit. Tough call. One answered by merlot. Inherent meatiness shepherds the subtle pork, its chocolate nuance plays up the sugar, sage and prunes, while structure contains the exuberance. Pork's common partner, pinot noir, is overwhelmed by this hot-pot.

wholegrain mustard is a mixture of ground and half-ground mustard seeds, which add an alluring texture and taste. The most famous grainy mustard is French *Moutarde de Meaux*, made from a closely-guarded secret recipe. It comes in wide-mouthed jars closed with sealing wax. There are lesser products about, so it's a good idea to seek out the best you can afford for this dish, as the flavour is extremely important.

This is one of those glorious one-pot dishes where the slow
simmering of ingredients results in subtle layers of flavours as
they mingle together. Bliss!

When it comes to the meat part of a posh meal, size does matter. With the increasing awareness of healthy eating, the idea that less (but better quality) is the way to go. Simple cooking methods for meat – grilling, frying, barbecuing, roasting – place a great deal of emphasis on quality, so source the best you can lay your hands on.

In the ways of the world, folk have different views on red meat, whether they be religious, ethical or health related. That said, it's a good idea to find out how the meat you're buying (and with which you're nourishing your nearest and dearest) has been farmed and treated before it reaches your table.

A good butcher is essential in the scheme of things, one who knows and understands meat and who (hopefully) is mindful of sound farming practises as well.

Lamb always conjures up images of feasts and religious celebrations – Easter in the Christian churches, the Eid festival marking the last month of the Muslim year, and Passover in the Jewish calendar.

Today's lamb (the meat of a sheep less than a year old) is bred way leaner than in times past, and should be served pink for tenderness, succulence and flavour. Mutton (from older sheep three to four years of age) prefers long, slow, moist cooking methods, and being served well done. Think slow-roasted Greek lamb with lashings of olive oil, garlic, rosemary, wine and citrus, and Moroccan Lamb Shanks with Coriander Yoghurt on page 136.

Hanging (maturing) lamb makes it more tender, and if your butcher hasn't done so already, you can do this at home. Choose large cuts with a good fat covering (not chops – they'll dry out), wipe with a vinegar-soaked cloth and place uncovered on a fridge shelf for between two to five days. For better browning, remember to bring lamb back to room temperature before cooking.

The phenomenal success of steakhouses, and their reputation of serving great steaks, is testimony to the quality of the product they promote: beef. The most highly-rated establishments go to great lengths to source the very best grainfed meat, which is what the home cook should do too.

If hanging is important to lamb, it's crucial to the taste and texture of beef. How long to hang? Many factors affect the issue, including temperature, air-flow and humidity, and even the experts can't reach consensus, agreeing as a rule of thumb upon anything between two and four weeks.

Ostrich, a popular alternative to red meat, provides a subtle taste of the wild. It's virtually fat free, low in cholesterol and kilojoules, while rich in protein. Though classified as game, it doesn't need to be marinated or hung. Since it has so little fat, which plays a significant role in the maturation of meat, it tends to mature quickly and is hence more perishable.

Venison is another matter entirely. Many parts of the world once teemed with an abundance of the wild wherewithal for a hearty meal. Sadly much has been decimated to near-extinction. Happily what's left is, for the most part, being treated with long overdue respect. But even the most intrepid cooks are terrified at the thought of preparing a venison meal; what guides us is usually a mixture of trial, error and disaster!

Experts agree that it's vital to hang venison, best accomplished by allowing the carcasses to languish quietly in a cool room for up to 14 days. If your meat comes from a hunting friend (who has, hopefully, bagged it with skill, also a factor in the quality of the meat), simply joint it (or you haven't a hope in hell of fitting it in the fridge) and lay uncovered on the rack.

Flavouring venison is a hotly debated topic and, though I adored my grandmother's way of studding it with bacon, tufts of rosemary and slivers of garlic, and cooking it in red wine, the truth is that it's simply not necessary – unless, of course, this is the way you like your venison cooked. If so, be my guest.

An even more sensitive subject – one that has caused more divorces than illicit affairs – is whether or not to marinate venison before cooking. Some of us wouldn't dream of subjecting a fine chunk of flesh to vinegar, wine and lemon juice, claiming they dry out the meat and affect the natural flavour. Others believe that venison should taste the way nature intended it to be.

Those averse to marinating venison (or beef or lamb, for that matter) immerse the meat in buttermilk for a day or so, which tenderizes it without affecting the flavour. And there's no law against flavouring the buttermilk with the likes of onion, garlic, crushed peppercorns and juniper berries. Or steep your meat in olive oil for a day or two. In terms of flavouring, the world is your oyster. Mint, garlic, ginger, rosemary and lavender spring to mind, as well as orange, lemon and lime, bacon, and spices like coriander, cinnamon and cumin.

moroccan lamb shanks
with coriander yoghurt

In their former life, lamb shanks were non-glam comfort zone family fare. Happily, the world
has rediscovered the joy of meat slow-cooked to the point where it literally falls off the bone.
Freshly-made masala adds a zing in this version that has greedy-guts appeal to spare.

serves 6

4 lamb shanks
sea salt and milled black pepper
olive oil
1 large onion, chopped
250ml (1 cup) beef stock (page 15)
250ml (1 cup) dry red wine
3–4 ripe tomatoes, blanched, peeled and chopped (see page 63)
finely grated zest of 1 small lemon
small bunch rosemary
5ml (1 teaspoon) green masala (see posh tip)
soft borrie maize meal, to serve (page 152)

coriander yoghurt
200ml (¾ cup) thick, plain yoghurt
small bunch coriander, chopped
freshly squeezed lemon juice

Season the lamb shanks with salt and pepper. Heat a little olive oil in a large ovenproof pan
and brown the meat well all over. Remove from the pan and set aside. Add the onion to the pan
and cook until golden (add a little more oil if necessary).

Add the stock, wine, tomatoes, lemon zest, rosemary and masala, then nestle in the shanks and
bring to the boil. Cover with the lid (or heavy foil) and bake for about 2 hours until the meat is
very tender. The cooking time depends on the size of the shanks, which should be turned from
time to time so they cook evenly.

coriander yoghurt While the lamb shanks are cooking, mix together the yoghurt and
coriander, and season with lemon juice and salt. (Add little crushed garlic too, if you wish.) Tip
into a small bowl and chill in the fridge.

to serve Lift the shanks from the sauce and place on a warm platter. If necessary, boil the
sauce uncovered to reduce and thicken, then pour over the meat. Serve with soft borrie maize
meal and chilled coriander yoghurt.

makeahead

Cook lamb shanks up to three days
ahead; store covered in the fridge.
Reheat gently on the stove-top or in
the oven. Coriander yoghurt is fine in
the fridge for a day.

poshtip

Freshly made masalas are hard to
find, so here's how to whip up your
own: pop 50g trimmed green (or red)
chillies into your food processor
with 30g scraped fresh ginger,
30g peeled garlic cloves, 2ml
(½ teaspoon) turmeric (borrie) and
45ml (3 tablespoons) vegetable oil.
Whizz to a paste, bottle and store in
the fridge. It will be fine for a week.

poshquaffing

Chilli-hot dishes are wine foe but
spices are another thing entirely.
Local Côtes-du-Rhone-styled reds
featuring shiraz, grenache and
pinotage (without obtrusive wood
tannins) support the food flavours
without clanking competition. Tinta
barocca proves too earthy, zinfandel
too jammy, so don't go that route.

masala-dusted ostrich steaks
with rosemary-balsamic glaze

This dish celebrates the glorious palette of Africa: one of it's favourite meats (ostrich) flavoured with a typical Cape Malay spice mix and sauced with a reduction of heady rosemary, balsamic vinegar and red wine. It's sure to break a vegetarian's heart!

serves 4

8 ostrich steaks, each about 100g
olive oil
roasted masala (page 24)
sea salt and milled black pepper

rosemary-balsamic glaze
125ml (½ cup) balsamic vinegar
60ml (4 tablespoons) sugar
leaves pulled from 3–4 rosemary sprigs
1 onion, roughly chopped
125ml (½ cup) dry red wine
60ml (¼ cup) cream
10ml (2 teaspoons) butter

Place the ostrich steaks in a dish and rub with olive oil. Sprinkle over a little roasted masala and press it into the surface. Set aside at room temperature for 3 to 4 hours (or overnight in the fridge), turning occasionally so the meat takes on the flavour of the masala.

rosemary-balsamic glaze Combine the balsamic vinegar, sugar and rosemary in a small saucepan. Bring to the boil, stirring to dissolve the sugar. Add the onion, cover and simmer very gently for about 10 minutes for the flavours to infuse. Uncover and boil briskly until reduced by half.

Strain the glaze into a clean saucepan. and press out all the moisture from the onion. Discard the onion and rosemary. Add the red wine and cream and simmer uncovered to reduce and thicken slightly. Whisk in the butter just before serving.

Heat a ridged grill-pan until searing hot, and grill the ostrich steaks for about 2 minutes on each side until well browned but still pink in the centre.

to serve Arrange the steaks on warm plates, season with salt and pepper, and drizzle with hot rosemary-balsamic glaze. Loads of crispy chips are the perfect partner.

makeahead

Ostrich needs to be rubbed with masala ahead of time, so arrange this to suit your schedule. Rosemary-balsamic glaze is quite happy if made a day ahead and reheated, but don't add the butter until just before serving.

poshtips

Ostrich has a high moisture content and very little fat compared to other meats, and special care is needed in cooking. Fry at high heat to seal in the juices and maintain succulence and flavour. An even better way is to barbecue the steaks over medium-hot coals.

poshquaffing

What other than a Cape blend for a dish so proudly South African – healthy ostrich, exotic Cape Malay spice and all? Usually pinotage-based, this accompaniment needs to be a lighter, less tannic style. Avoid top-end stuff – unless somebody else is buying, then compromise food and wine matrimony and get as much bliss in a glass as you can.

Ostrich steaks are often referred to as 'fillet', but it's not really so, for the bird has no fillet, but muscle which looks, tastes and is cooked like beef fillet.

mauritian beef rougail
with cucumber dhal

serves 4

cucumber dhal
½ English cucumber
250ml (1 cup) thick, plain yoghurt
½ small green chilli, sliced, seeded and very finely chopped
small bunch coriander, finely chopped

600g fillet, rump or sirloin steak
6 garlic cloves, peeled
2cm piece fresh ginger, scraped and roughly chopped
1 red or green chilli, seeded and roughly chopped
5 curry leaves
leaves from a bunch thyme (about 45ml/3 tablespoons leaves)
2ml (½ teaspoon) turmeric (borrie)
30ml (2 tablespoons) tomato purée
vegetable oil
sea salt and milled black pepper
1 large onion, finely sliced
400g small, ripe tomatoes, halved or quartered
250ml (1 cup) beef stock (page 15)
small bunch coriander, roughly chopped
4–5 spring onions, trimmed and finely sliced

cucumber dhal Grate the cucumber coarsely (leave the skin on) and pile into a sieve placed over a bowl. Leave for about 30 minutes to drain; shake occasionally. Tip into a bowl, season with salt, and mix in the yoghurt, chilli and coriander. Cover and chill in the fridge.

Trim the steak and cut into large chunks. Pound together the garlic, ginger and chilli in a pestle and mortar. Mix in the curry leaves, thyme, turmeric and tomato purée.

Heat a little oil in a large frying pan and brown the meat over very high heat. Set aside and season lightly with salt and pepper. Add a little more oil to the pan and fry the onion until golden. Add the garlic and ginger paste, tomatoes and stock, and cook uncovered for about 3 minutes until the sauce thickens nicely. Check the flavour – you may like to add more salt and pepper as well as a little sugar to balance the acidity of the tomatoes.

Return the meat to the pan and simmer gently (still uncovered) for about 5 minutes; the steak should be medium-rare. Remove from the heat and mix in the coriander.

to serve Transfer the rougail to a large platter, and tart it up to the nines with a profusion of spring onion. Serve with rice and cucumber dhal.

makeahead

The whole idea is for rougail to be served fresh from the pan. To pre-prepare, cook to the stage when the meat is returned to the sauce. Reheat, and stir in the coriander just before serving. Cucumber dhal may be prepared up to three days ahead; keep covered in the fridge.

poshtip

The most definitive ingredient in a rougail is fresh tomato. Sadly, the glorious, flavoursome *pomme d'amour* aren't piled high in our markets as they are in Port Louis, but roma, rosa and cherry tomatoes may be substituted. Just make sure they're ripe as can be and bursting with flavour.

poshquaffing

As 'rustic' and 'refined' are juxtaposed on the plate, so too they need to be in the glass. Shiraz has enough spicy oomph to dance with the Créole seasoning, but stand-alone bottlings dominate. When blended with meaty merlot, the match is just right. Other Bordeaux varieties (cabernet) are too linear; even fully wooded chardonnay is blown away.

Take a ladleful of French flair and a pinch of Chinese mystery, add a dash of Indian spice and African allure and what do you get? Marvellous, multi-faceted Mauritian cuisine, a mix of rustic simplicity and sophisticated refinement. The rougail (or rougaille) zings with the passion of the island, and it's amongst the memorable Créole dishes I enjoyed during many visits there.

beef fillet
with slow-roasted onions and garlic

serves 6 to 8

slow-roasted onions and garlic
750g pickling onions, skinned
2 garlic heads
30ml (2 tablespoons) chopped rosemary needles

1,5 kg whole fillet steak
sea salt and milled black pepper
olive oil
60ml (¼ cup) water
125ml (½ cup) brandy

slow-roasted onions and garlic Heat the oven to 180ºC. Scatter the onions into a roasting pan. Cut the tops off the garlic heads, separate the cloves (don't peel them), and add to the pan. Toss rosemary on top and season with salt and pepper. Drizzle liberally with olive oil and roast uncovered for about 50 minutes until golden and tender, sweet and caramelized. Turn occasionally in the oil.

Trim the meat and season with plenty of pepper and a little salt. To pan-roast: heat a little oil in a large saucepan. Brown on all sides over high heat, then reduce the heat to medium, add the water and cover with a well-fitting lid (if yours is dodgy, add a layer of heavy foil to seal nicely). Pan-roast the meat, turning every few minutes so it cooks evenly. The total cooking time should not exceed 20 minutes for fillet that is rare in the centre, graduating to medium at each end.

Just before removing the steak from the pan, pour over the brandy and flame. Allow the flames to die down. Lift the fillet onto a warm plate, tent loosely with foil and rest for about 10 minutes. Meanwhile, boil the pan juices uncovered until reduced and thickened.

To barbecue: When your coals are hot and ready for action, rub the fillet with olive oil and brown well on all sides. Then raise the grid from the heat and cook at a more moderate rate. It will be medium-rare in about 40 minutes, with an internal temperature of 60ºC on a meat thermometer.

to serve Carve the fillet into thick slices and arrange on a warm plate. Pour over the reduced pan juices (if you've pan-roasted the steak) and surround with slow-roasted onions and garlic.

makeahead
Slow-roasted onions and garlic may be prepared up to a day ahead; reheat just before serving. Fillet must be pan-roasted or barbecued just before serving.

posh**tip**
Garlic roasted long and slow is tender and aromatic and has a mellow, sweet flavour, unlike the sharpness of the raw stuff.

posh**quaffing**
Cabernet sauvignon. Well, yes and no. The king of red wines is beef's classic match, but less forgiving with the sweet, caramelized garlic and onions. This is the domain of ripe merlot and other bits and bobs that soften the mainstay in Bordeaux-style blends – our choice. Plump pinotage and sensorial shiraz are just too awkward and adolescent.

Roasting or barbecuing a whole beef fillet is the way to go when tastes vary. The plump mid-section remains rare, while thinner end slices will be better done for those who like it this way. Ascertain preferences beforehand and adjust the cooking time accordingly.

north african veal casserole
with onions and feta

This gutsy, lusty dish will cheer you up when the weather's not as sunny and warm as hoped. And even though it's not quick to cook, at least is does so without demanding any intervention from the cook, simmering away on the stove while you get on with something else.

serves 6

1,2 kg veal knuckle
sea salt and milled black pepper
vegetable oil
1 large onion, roughly chopped
500ml (1 cup) beef stock (page 15), or half beef stock, half red wine
500g ripe tomatoes, blanched, skinned and chopped (see page 63)
  or 400g tin tomatoes, chopped in their juice
15ml (1 tablespoon) brown sugar
1 bunch herbs (bay leaf, parsley, thyme, oregano)
5ml (1 teaspoon) ground cumin
1ml (¼ teaspoon) ground cloves
1 cinnamon stick
750g pickling onions, skinned
100g feta cheese, crumbled

Trim the meat and season with salt and pepper. Heat a little oil in a large saucepan and brown the meat in batches. Add the chopped onion to the pan and fry until golden.

Tip the meat back into the pan with the stock, tomato, sugar, herbs, cumin, cloves and cinnamon. Season with salt and pepper, cover and simmer very gently for about 1½ hours until tender. Add the pickling onions, cover and simmer for about 20 minutes until they're done.

to serve This looks great served in individual pans. Alternatively, transfer to a warm platter and garnish with crumbled feta. Rice or mashed potato are good accompaniments.

makeahead

Casseroles are perfect for making ahead; flavours are even more unctuous if they have time to spend in each others' company. Chill in the fridge for a day or two, and reheat very gently in the oven or on the stove-top.

poshtip

If there's no veal knuckle to be had, use stewing lamb or beef instead. The cooking time may vary, so keep an eye on it.

poshquaffing

Shiraz, on both paper and the plate. Rich flavours of tomato, garlic, bay leaf, cumin, cinnamon and cloves understudy the casserole but direct the wine partner. Gear up with single varietal versions offering elegant fruit and a touch of spice. Warmer blends and plummy pinotage risk being trenchant.

pepper-crust venison
with orange and honey sauce

South Africans love to filch the flavours from their neighbours and are passionate about mixing sweet and savoury tastes in one dish. This evocative orange and honey sauce borrows tastes from North Africa. Use sparingly as the flavour is powerful.

serves 4 to 6

600–700g whole springbok loin (in one piece)
olive oil and butter
sea salt and milled black pepper
chilli-ginger broccoli, to serve (page 150)

orange and honey sauce
15ml (1 tablespoon) cumin seeds
15ml (1 tablespoon) scraped and grated fresh ginger
500ml (2 cups) orange juice
finely grated zest and juice of 1 lemon
80ml (⅓ cup) clear honey

Trim the meat and cut it in half if necessary, to fit your pan. Place in a dish, rub well with olive oil and season generously with pepper.

orange and honey sauce Roast the cumin seeds in a dry frying pan until toasty and aromatic. Allow to cool, then pound with the ginger in a pestle and mortar. Tip into a medium saucepan and add the orange juice, lemon zest and juice, ginger and honey. Boil uncovered, stirring occasionally, until reduced by two-thirds. Strain into a jug, pressing out all the moisture.

To pan-roast the meat: heat a generous amount of olive oil and butter in a frying pan, add the venison and brown well all over. Cover and roast over more gentle heat. It should be served rare, so about 5 minutes' cooking should be enough; add a few minutes more in you prefer your meat more well done.

To barbecue: grill the meat on an oiled grid over hot coals until well browned on all sides. Raise the grid from the heat and cook over more moderate heat for 6 to 8 minutes.

Lift the meat from the pan (or grid) onto a board, tent with foil and allow to rest for about 10 minutes.

to serve Slice the venison fairly thinly and arrange on a platter. Serve with orange and honey sauce and chilli-ginger broccoli. For a posher presentation, serve with two sauces: the one suggested here, and rosemary-balsamic glaze on page 38.

makeahead

Venison may be oiled and peppered a couple of hours ahead. Keep covered and refrigerated. Orange and honey sauce is fine for a day. Even the broccoli is no problem; it tastes great at room temperature, so prepare a couple of hours before serving.

poshtip

Despite the fact that venison loin is often erroneously referred to as 'fillet', a saddle has the loin on the upper side and the smaller fillets underneath. Other antelope that are good in this recipe include impala, gemsbok and kudu.

poshquaffing

Pinotage may not be the tipple of choice on the Karoo plains where springbok roam, but it's born to accompany this creation. More serious bottlings add breadth to the lean meat and, most tellingly, counter the sweet/spicy sauce while coping with the chilli-ginger side dish. Avoid lesser fruity offerings or easy Med-red blends – they're too clumsy in the match.

Venison is easy to cook, despite the perception that it takes skill. That said, it's true that the mere thought of preparing venison is enough to strike terror in the heart of the most expert cook.

Here's a fresh look at ways to serve **side dishes** prepared from the lovely stuff we pick, pluck and pull from the ground – or purchase neatly wrapped, loose or in bunches from our favourite farmstall. Glorious vegetables richly deserve more than a passing glance.

I was raised on vegetables at their seasonal best, thanks to rotating crops from our small farm. I still find it hard to resist shopping at farmers' markets: carrots and potatoes damp from the earth; bunches of bright, proud spinach; leeks with roots; tomatoes ripened on the vine. These are sights, smells and tastes of my childhood that I still find utterly irresistible.

When it comes to posh side dishes, it's time to rediscover the joy of produce that's local and in season, rather than goodies flown in from another part of the world. Visit the market rather than the supermarket. Grow your own herbs – they don't need much space – find a sunny corner in the garden or place a row of pots on the window sill.

Better still, allocate an area for planting a few rows of vegetables. Gardening is great for the soul (not to mention the waistline), and does wonders for the sense of humour when the rigours of the day leave you stressed out. Home-grown food is addictive.

Keep an open mind when shopping for vegetables. Allow yourself to be seduced by what you see, and be creative. Even if you've meticulously listed all the stuff specified in the recipe you plan to make, change your shopping list.

Be single-minded about sourcing perfect greens. Insist on the freshest salad leaves, find onions that deliver punch without bitter pungency, mushrooms with texture and flavour, carrots with crunch, slender, young brinjals that are firm and less likely to be bitter.

I subscribe to the belief that greens are good for you: there's always one to suit your mood, menu and pocket. Think brussels sprouts, spinach, cabbage, broccoli, chicory, pak choi ... the list goes on forever and a day.

To make everything taste as fresh as can be, tamper with them as little as possible. In general, vegetables respond best to simple treatment and few embellishments. Serve them in the way nature intended, and avoid turning, twisting or (heaven forbid!) bundling them up with chives. Leave such time-consuming tasks to chefs on ego trips and kitchen help to spare.

Time spent in boarding school convinced me that water is anathema to green vegetables. Rather choose steam, oil or butter to wilt them in; add judicious amounts of salt and pepper, a touch of sugar or chilli if you wish, and generous quantities of garlic and fresh herbs. Do please avoid cooking greens to a mushy anonymity. Not all vegetables are best when they're undercooked, though – onions and leeks need time to make them lusciously unctuous, and gently and sweetly caramelized on the edges. Brinjals need to be meltingly tender. Mushrooms and corn meanwhile, must be cooked just so: tender to the bite but not too floppy.

Don't skimp on the cooking time of root vegetables like parsnips, turnips, carrots and beetroot, which are at their best roasted long and slow, with oodles of moisture – olive oil, butter and maybe a splash of water to create steam – and flavourings of ginger, garlic, honey or brown sugar, and masses of garlic.

Potatoes, to my mind, are kings of the kitchen. There's nothing quite as satisfying as new potatoes boiled in their skins and rolled in butter (or not!) or a baked potato, crisp skin crackling with olive oil and sea salt, split to reveal its fluffy tummy oozing enticingly with a splodge of sour cream or crème fraîche, and perhaps a little crumbled blue cheese. Bliss! But this is only the start of their recipe repertoire: potatoes may be roasted, chipped or sautéed; sliced, layered with cream, crushed garlic and grated parmesan and baked until they collapse; grated and fried into cakes; boiled and mashed with butter and cream or olive oil, and flavoured with chives, parmesan, garlic, bacon or spiced, fried onion. All are out of this world.

The recipes that follow are designed as sides to some of the main courses in our book. Yet they are so delicious that – mixed and matched – they're perfect with a roast or as an adjunct to a barbecue, and will impress the vegetarians at your table no end.

chilli-ginger broccoli

serves 4 to 6

300g young, long-stemmed broccoli
1 chilli, seeded and very finely chopped
3–4 garlic cloves, peeled and crushed
5ml (1 teaspoon) grated fresh ginger
125ml (½ cup) olive oil
30ml (2 tablespoons) soy sauce
small bunch coriander, roughly chopped

Trim the broccoli, then steam over boiling water until tender; don't overcook – it should be slightly crunchy to the bite. Arrange on a plate.

While the broccoli is steaming, prepare the dressing. Mix together the chilli, garlic, ginger, olive oil and soy sauce in a jug. Mix in the chopped coriander. Pour the dressing over the hot broccoli.

Serve this flavourful vegetable dish at room temperature garnished, if wished, with extra coriander sprigs which will improve both the look and taste.

saffron-glazed carrots

serves 4 to 6

600g small, slim carrots
50g butter
2 star anise
few threads saffron or
   1ml (¼ teaspoon) turmeric (borrie)
sea salt and milled black pepper
15ml (1 tablespoon) demerara sugar
125ml (½ cup) vegetable stock (page 15)

Wash the carrots and trim the stalks so they look good when you serve them. Heat the butter in a large frying pan with the star anise and saffron or turmeric, then add the carrots, turning them in the butter to coat evenly. Season with a little salt and pepper, and cook slowly uncovered for about 10 minutes (depending on size) until half cooked. Roll them around from time to time so they cook evenly.

Sprinkle the sugar onto the carrots and turn until lightly glazed. Pour in the stock and cook more briskly, still uncovered, until the sauce has reduced to a light glaze and the carrots are cooked. Serve hot.

creamed cauliflower

serves 4

500g cauliflower, roughly chopped
500ml (2 cups) milk
125ml (½ cup) cream
sea salt and milled black pepper
grated nutmeg

Put the cauliflower into a medium saucepan with the milk and cream, and a pinch of salt, pepper and nutmeg. Simmer gently uncovered for about 15 minutes until the cauliflower is very soft and the liquid has reduced by half. Drain the cauliflower; reserve the liquid.

Measure 150ml of the liquid, pour into a food processor with the cauliflower. Whizz fairly smoothly, adding more liquid if necessary. Reheat and serve hot.

roasted tomatoes and peppers

serves 4

2 large, ripe tomatoes, cut into quarters
2 red or yellow peppers, cored
 and cut into quarters
6 garlic cloves, peeled and chopped
60ml (4 tablespoons) olive oil
sea salt and milled black pepper
12 basil leaves, roughly torn

Set the oven at 200ºC. Arrange the tomatoes and peppers in a roasting dish to fit them snugly in a single layer. Scatter over the garlic, drizzle with olive oil and season generously with salt and pepper.

Place in the oven, switch on the grill and grill the vegetables for about 10 minutes until tender and slightly charred.

Scatter over the basil and serve the vegetables straight from the roaster, or arrange on a serving dish. Serve warm or at room temperature.

corn cakes

serves 6 to 8

340g tin cream-style sweetcorn
1 egg, lightly beaten
5ml (1 teaspoon) dijon mustard
125ml (½ cup) cake flour
2ml (½ teaspoon) baking powder
sea salt and milled black pepper
grated nutmeg
vegetable oil

Shortly before you plan to fry the corn cakes, mix together the corn, egg and mustard in a bowl. Sift in the flour and baking powder, season with salt, pepper and a little nutmeg, and mix well.

Make eight corn cakes: fry spoonfuls of the batter in hot oil in a frying pan until crisp on both sides and cooked right through. If insufficiently cooked, the fritters will be runny in the middle.

Drain well on kitchen paper, then arrange on a hot plate. Serve warm.

brandied butternut

serves 6

1 medium butternut, about 800g
60ml (¼ cup) water
50g butter
30ml (2 tablespoons) clear honey
45ml (3 tablespoons) brandy
finely grated zest of 1 small lemon

Set the oven at 200ºC. Peel and pip the butternut and slice lengthwise into slim strips. Arrange in a single layer in a baking dish to fit snugly.

Combine the water, butter, honey, brandy and lemon zest in a small saucepan, heat until melted, then pour over the butternut. Cover with foil and bake for about 30 minutes until soft. Remove the foil, baste the butternut with the buttery brandy sauce and turn on the grill to sizzle the surface toasty-brown.

soft borrie maize meal

serves 6 to 8

750ml (3 cups) vegetable stock (page 15)
1ml (¼ teaspoon) turmeric (borrie)
2ml (½ teaspoon) sea salt
200ml (¾ cup) maize meal
125ml (½ cup) cream (approximate amount)

Bring the stock to the boil in a medium saucepan. Add the turmeric and salt, then slowly stir in the maize meal. Cook over very low heat for about 5 minutes, stirring frequently. Stir in the cream, cover and set aside for an hour or more to thicken.

Reheat the maize meal just before serving and check the consistency; you may need to add a little more cream.

maize meal wedges

serves 6

1 litre (4 cups) vegetable stock (page 15)
5ml (1 teaspoon) sea salt
500ml (2 cups) maize meal
50g butter, melted, plus extra for greasing
   the baking sheet

Bring the stock to the boil with the salt in a large saucepan. Tip in the maize meal, stir briskly to mix thoroughly, cover and cook undisturbed over gentle heat for about 20 minutes. Spread the maize meal onto a buttered baking sheet to a thickness of approximately 2cm and allow to cool.

Cut the maize meal into neat wedges, brush liberally with melted butter and place under a preheated oven grill until hot, crisp and golden brown.

curried pulses

serves 6 to 8

1 red onion, finely sliced
olive oil
400g tin brown lentils, drained
5ml (1 teaspoon) roasted masala (page 24),
   or curry powder
425g tin chickpeas, drained
sea salt and milled black pepper
15ml (1 tablespoon) balsamic vinegar
30ml (2 tablespoons) chopped mint leaves

Gently fry the onion in olive oil in a large saucepan until golden. Stir in the masala or curry powder, then add the lentils and chickpeas and heat through. Season with salt and pepper.

Remove from the heat and stir in the balsamic vinegar and mint. Set aside for an hour or two (overnight is even better) before serving, to allow the flavours to infuse.

Transfer the curried pulses to a bowl and serve at room temperature.

spicy mashed potato

serves 4 to 6

4 large potatoes, peeled and diced
sea salt and milled black pepper
olive oil
4 cardamom pods, lightly crushed
2 onions, finely sliced
1 small green chilli, finely sliced
freshly squeezed lemon juice
small bunch coriander, roughly chopped

Cook the potatoes in salted boiling water until soft. Drain off most of the liquid, season with salt and pepper and mash with a little olive oil until nice and creamy.

Heat a generous glug of olive oil in a frying pan until it sizzles, add the cardamom, then the onion and chilli and fry until the onion is well browned. Mix in the mashed potato and a little lemon juice and heat through. Just before serving, gently mix in the chopped coriander.

This dish may be made a day ahead and reheated, but don't add the coriander until shortly before serving, as it will lose all its appeal – not to mention colour and taste.

herb-crushed spuds

serves 6 to 8

800g potatoes
100g butter
olive oil
small bunch spring onions, trimmed
    and sliced
sea salt and milled black pepper
125ml (½ cup) chopped herbs (parsley,
    marjoram, oregano, fennel)

Boil the potatoes in their jackets until half cooked (if they're mushy before the frying starts, you'll end up with mash). Drain, peel and cut into chunks.

Sizzle the butter in a large frying pan, then add a splash of olive oil (don't be mean with the amount; it's vital for the flavour and crustiness of the potatoes.) Stir in the spring onion, then add the potato chunks and season with salt and pepper. Fry until crisp and golden, turning occasionally at the start, and more frequently as the potatoes get crisp and crunchy. Try not to mash them too much – this will spoil the effect completely – and add more olive oil if needs be. Stir in the herbs and transfer the potatoes to a serving plate. Serve hot.

wine-glazed new potatoes

serves 4 to 5

750g new potatoes, well scrubbed
200ml (¾ cup) dry white wine
sea salt and milled black pepper
30ml (2 tablespoons) chopped
    flat-leaf parsley
50g butter

Boil the potatoes in their jackets in salted water until soft. Drain well, then tip into a large frying pan. Add the wine and season with salt and pepper. Boil uncovered until the liquid has reduced to a glaze and the potatoes are well flavoured, turning them in the pan-juices from time to time.

Add the parsley and butter, shaking the pan until the butter melts. In a wonderfully forgiving way, these potatoes taste fabulous freshly-cooked or when they have cooled down. You choose!

Here, with bags of love, is my favourite part of the book,

one that will answer all your questions about

perfect posh **endings**.

Dessert is the best part of the menu, the dish you'll

remember long after you've left the table,

so pull out all the stops.

We all know that heart-health matters, but this doesn't mean

that we shouldn't occasionally throw caution to the wind and

indulge in a little something diet-defying and utterly delicious.

This is no time to be parsimonious about sinful, sensual

ingredients like chocolate, cream and eggs. You can compensate

by helping yourself to the teeniest portion possible.

I'm an unrepentant chocoholic, and have been passionate about dessert for as long as I can remember. As a child, sweets and chocolates were occasional treats, but there was always a bowl of chocolate pudding in the fridge (custard made with creamy milk, farm eggs and cocoa), and it was trotted out at every meal – occasionally even for breakfast. If you haven't sprinkled cornflakes onto chocolate pudding, you haven't lived!

At other times, a slice of bread spread with butter sprinkled liberally with sugar would suffice (it's still my favourite midnight munchie), but this will hardly do at a more larney dinner.

The hardest part is deciding what to make, but when you've made up your mind and done the shopping, it's plain sailing from there on. Consider the meal as a whole before deciding on how it should end. Lighter meals can cope with more fulsome desserts involving cream, chocolate and eggs; a heavier menu would be happier with something light and fruity.

Cheese is perfect to nibble on while finishing off the last of the red wine and before heading in the direction of the sweet part of the menu and dessert wine. Choose just one type – brie, camembert, gorgonzola, blue cheese, goat's cheese, you name it – or offer a selection. Serve solo, or with biscuits, bread or fruit.

When shopping for cheese, make sure it's perfectly ripe and purchase in small amounts so that it won't languish too long in the fridge. Wrap well, keep in the vegetable storage where it is not too cold, and always bring to room temperature before serving.

A heavenly idea is to unwrap a wedge of brie or a whole camembert, place in a dish and warm in the oven until it oozes and is on the edge of melting. Some crusty bread alongside is all you need.

My best puds are those that can be made ahead and whipped onto the table with minimum fuss and bother. Of course, if you're in the mood to cook yourself into a frenzy preparing all manner of complicated recipes, be my guest (there are loads of fabulous ideas in the pages that follow).

Sweet-tooths can be satisfied with very little: a perfect piece of fruit, drippingly ripe and smelling like heaven, a bowl of cherries drizzled with a little berry-based liqueur, apple wedges roasted in a hot oven with butter and brown sugar, and topped with warm custard.

If it all seems too much and you can't be bothered to trawl through recipes and prepare one from scratch, pile a selection of chocolates and other sweet treats into your prettiest bowl and pass it around. Not only will it be a conversation-stopper, but it will satisfy all those who can't do without their sugar fix.

Finally, here are some quick and easy after-the-meal ideas for short-order cooks.

Brie and preserved figs

Cheese are fruit are soul-mates: think cheddar and apples; blue cheese and ripe peaches or nectarines; mascarpone and fresh figs (plus a drizzle of honey for good measure); parmesan and pears; goat's cheese and summer berries. Cheese with preserves of any kind – especially figs – makes everyone happy. Ripe brie is the best choice (offer a selection of cheeses if you feel like pulling out all the stops). Then simply drain a jar of preserved figs and arrange them artfully on a plate, with a sprig of garden greenery for good measure. No stress, no fuss, and a minimum of skill required in the presentation.

ice-cream and hot chocolate sauce

King of desserts, cornerstone of edible depravity, thing of beauty and a joy forever. Unless, of course, it has been prepared with ingredients that are less than perfect. Chocolate stimulates the brain centres and releases sensual pleasure hormones. Sure, it's fattening, but this fact cuts no ice when the devil inside urges you to indulge.

- **ice-cream (the best you can find!)**
- **200g good quality dark chocolate, roughly chopped**
- **100g Mars Bar or Bar One, roughly chopped**
- **60ml (4 tablespoons) cream**
- **30ml (2 tablespoons) chocolate, citrus or coffee-based liqueur (optional)**

Scoop the ice-cream into balls, and pile them back into the container or into a serving bowl. Return to the freezer until serving time. Combine the remaining ingredients in a bowl and melt in a pan of simmering water. Stir until smooth, then pour into a bowl or jug. Serves 6

biscotti and sweet wine

Source the very best biscotti on the market, and offer with a glass of well-chilled dessert wine of your choice. Invite everyone to dip the biscuits into the wine, and nibble them as they start to soften. Heaven!

strawberries with balsamic vinegar and pepper

A blissful marriage! Simply purchase the ripest strawberries you can lay your hands on, rinse them, and pile into a beautiful glass bowl. Just before serving, anoint with a few twists of the peppermill and a sprinkling of balsamic vinegar. A selection of cheeses alongside would be good as well.

sozzled nectarines
with pinotage and lavender

Fragrant nectarines are one of summer's greatest pleasures. In this voluptuous recipe they're poached in wine syrup fragrant with honey and lavender. If nectarines aren't in season, use peaches, pears or plums instead.

serves 8

8 ripe nectarines
375ml (1½ cups) pinotage (or another dry red wine)
375ml (1½ cups) water
125ml (½ cup) sugar
60ml (4 tablespoons) clear honey
1 lime, sliced
small bunch lavender (leaves and flowers)
mascarpone cheese or whipped cream, to serve

Peel the nectarines and prick all over with a skewer so they absorb the flavours of the poaching liquid as they cook.

Choose a medium saucepan to fit the fruit snugly and combine the wine, water, sugar, honey, lime slices and lavender. Stir over medium heat until the sugar has dissolved, then bring the syrup to the boil.

Add the nectarines to the pan, cover and poach until nice and tender. This will take no more than 10 minutes, depending on how ripe they are.

Lift the fruit into a bowl. Simmer the syrup uncovered until reduced by half and slightly thickened. Strain over the nectarines and allow to cool. Chill in the fridge.

to serve Serve your sozzled nectarines at room temperature. A spoonful of mascarpone or whipped cream rounds things off deliciously.

make ahead

Sozzled nectarines are even better a couple of days after being prepared. Bring to room temperature; the flavour is more striking than when they're chilled.

posh quaffing

Pinotage. Seriously. No, not the dry red wine, rather the Cape's version of Pineau des Charentes, basically a fortified grape-must in jerepigo style. It matches the palate without cloying. For less hectic times and to unveil the lavender, sparkling dry rosé reflects the hues and lifts the ensemble with just enough fruit to hold its own. Refreshing too.

Nectarines are smooth-skinned and rosy-cheeked, and there's nothing quite as heavenly as munching them messily – skin and all – when they're fully, fragrantly ripe. If you'd rather use peaches, make sure they're the soft, freestone type. Unlike clingstone peaches, the flesh comes away easily and cleanly from the stone; way more luscious to my mind.

Present this pud prettily, partner it with the perfect wine, and you'll be amply rewarded.

bali-style pears and berries
with honey-cinnamon yoghurt

Although Bali doesn't pretend to be a gourmet destination, the islanders' way with fruit is memorable, and inspired this summery pudding which looks as divine as it tastes. Choose your favourite berries and, if fresh ones aren't available, frozen berries will do; defrost on a wad of kitchen paper to absorb excess moisture.

serves 8

500g mixed berries
8 pears
750ml (3 cups) water
250ml (1 cup) sugar
1 lemon, sliced
5ml (1 teaspoon) vanilla extract
1 cinnamon stick
3 whole cloves
3 star anise
2 stalks lemon grass, cut in half lengthwise

honey-cinnamon yoghurt
250ml (1 cup) thick, plain yoghurt
15ml (1 tablespoon) clear honey
2ml (½ teaspoon) ground cinnamon

Pile the berries into a colander and rinse under running water (don't soak them as this may make them mushy). Tip into a bowl, cover and chill while poaching the pears.

Peel the pears and core from the base with a corer or knife. Cut in half if you wish; they'll cook quicker, but won't look as dramatic as whole pears.

Combine the water, sugar, lemon slices, vanilla, cinnamon, cloves, star anise and lemon grass in a saucepan that fits the pears snugly. Bring to the boil. Add the pears, cover and simmer for about 40 minutes until tender when pierced with a skewer. (Halved pears will cook in about 30 minutes.) Turn in the syrup occasionally so they cook evenly. Remove from the heat, add the berries and allow the fruit to cool in the syrup.

honey-cinnamon yoghurt Mix the ingredients together in a bowl.

to serve This pretty pud looks best in glass bowls or glasses. Top each serving with a spoonful of honey-cinnamon yoghurt.

makeahead
The pears may be cooked up to three days ahead. Berries are fine in the fridge for a day; add to the syrup shortly before serving. Honey-cinnamon yoghurt may be refrigerated for a day at the most.

poshtips
For maximum visual appeal, use mixed berries; small strawberries, raspberries, boysenberries, youngberries, tayberries and gooseberries. Instead of honey-cinnamon yoghurt, you could offer chilled mascarpone cheese or crème fraîche.

poshquaffing
From Bali to the Eastern Cape, where traditional honey beer – mead – is being commercially produced as 'Iqhilika'. Surprisingly dry, with all the richness of honey without the sweetness, its fragrance alone is just desserts for this fab finale. Gewürztraminer in special late harvest style is an alternative to match the fruit/yoghurt combo.

Bali is one of the Indonesian islands which, for two thousand years, have been at the crossroads of world trade. This accounts for the diverse culinary influences from India, China, Arabia, Europe and Malaysia which features a liberal use of spices.

almond pavlovas
with orange compôte

Mention meringues and all resistance crumbles; they're fabulous, frivolous and fun to eat. Forget those awful store-bought crisp numbers produced by a piping bag (and a chef with no soul); our free-form pavlovas with soft centres look like floaty clouds. A tangy compôte completes the pretty picture.

serves 10

4 egg whites
250g castor sugar
15ml (1 tablespoon) cornflour
7ml (1½ teaspoons) white wine vinegar
2ml (½ teaspoon) vanilla extract
50g flaked almonds

orange compôte
6 oranges
45ml (3 tablespoons) sugar
15ml (1 tablespoon) cornflour
30ml (2 tablespoons) water

Heat the oven to 200ºC. Line a large baking tray with foil and spray lightly with oil. Beat the egg whites with an electric mixer until very stiff. Add the castor sugar a few tablespoons at a time, beating well between each addition. Mix the cornflour into the last measure of sugar. Add the vinegar and vanilla extract, and beat for a few minutes more until the meringue is thick and glossy.

Lift ten large spoonfuls onto the baking tray; don't make the mounds too smooth. Scatter the almonds on top. Bake in the centre of the oven for approximately 5 minutes until the pavlovas are tinged with brown, then reduce the heat to 100ºC and bake for a further 30 minutes. Switch off the heat and cool the pavlovas in the oven.

orange compôte Finely grate the zest of one orange. Peel and segment all the oranges, and place in a bowl. Squeeze the juice from the skins into a medium saucepan and add the orange zest and sugar. Bring to the boil, stirring constantly, until the sugar dissolves. Mix together the cornflour and water, add and boil until the sauce is clear and thickened. Mix in the fruit segments and allow the compôte to cool.

to serve Place the pavlovas on plates and spoon compôte alongside, or present on a huge platter with mint sprigs here and there for more visual drama.

makeahead

Like all meringues, pavlovas keep beautifully. Cool then pack in an airtight container and store in a dry spot (not in the fridge) for up to a week. Orange compôte may be made up to three days ahead; keep covered and chilled in the fridge.

poshtip

Forego the fruity part of the recipe and offer lashings of whipped cream instead.

poshquaffing

After all manner of trials with sweet reds, full muscadels and noble late harvest wines, gently off-dry muscat (de Frontignan, d'Alexandrie) comes out tops. Not too sweet to clash with meringue, its tangerine twist echoes the compôte while sparring with almond nuttiness. Super-chilled white port is for the adventurous.

old cape
crusty custard

Sweet-tooths get moist-eyed at very idea of this fabulously rich custard with its distinctive burnt sugar capping. This version of crème brûlée has the added zing of the Cape's famous liqueur, Van der Hum, made from fine South African brandy flavoured with tangerines (locally known as naartjies). If you don't relish the idea of messing about with the classics, simply leave out the booze.

serves 6 to 8

500ml (2 cups) cream
250ml (1 cup) full cream milk
finely grated zest of ½ lemon
6 egg yolks
80ml (⅓ cup) castor sugar
5ml (1 teaspoon) vanilla extract
60ml (4 tablespoons) Van der Hum liqueur
castor sugar, for the topping

Set the oven at 160ºC. Heat the cream, milk and lemon zest in a medium saucepan to just below boiling point.

Whisk together the egg yolks and castor sugar. Stir in the hot cream. Pour back into the pan and cook over low heat, stirring constantly, until the custard thickens and coats the spoon. Remove from the heat and stir in the vanilla extract and Van der Hum.

Strain the custard into a jug, then pour into ovenproof bowls (teacups work well) and bake in a bain-marie for about 30 minutes until set. Remove the bowls (or cups) from the water bath and chill in the fridge.

to serve Sprinkle a layer of castor sugar onto the surface of the custards and glaze with a blowtorch or under a hot oven grill until crisp, crusty and caramelized.

makeahead

Bake the custards a couple of days ahead of time, allow to cool, then cover with clingfilm and refrigerate. Caramelize the sugar within a few hours of serving or it will get sticky; it can happily languish in the fridge for an hour or two.

poshtip

You could also use icing sugar for the topping. Torch it in two layers, chilling in between, for the crunchiest result.

poshquaffing

As a complement, chilled cream liqueur adds to the baked custard powerhouse, all cut by Van der Hum's citric tang. Keep it 'Cape' – South African rather – with Amarula. In contrast, a natural sweet wine (chenin blanc, semillon) has sufficient fruit to share. Anything more austere ruins the decadence.

van der hum, sweet golden mystery in a tiny glass, originated as a 7th century family recipe for which a wine merchant paid the princely sum of 800 pounds. There were eventually some 20 Van der Hum distillers in the Cape, one of whom is reported to have used 8 000 baskets of fresh naartjies every year for his brew. Some say it was named after an Admiral Van der Hum in the Dutch East India Company's fleet who was particularly fond of it. If you can't find the specified liqueur, use any citrus-based liqueur such as Cointreau, Curaçao or Grand Marnier.

The origins of the recipe for crème brûlée are controversial, to say the least. France insists it originated there; others maintain it's a speciality of New Orleans (and I sampled heavenly southern-style renditions of it in my travels in that part of the world). My stern Scottish grandfather insisted that a Scot brought it to Cambridge from Aberdeenshire in the 1860s and introduced it into Trinity College. In my wildest dreams I would never even argue the point.

rice pudding with attitude
and fried pineapple

serves 4

125ml (½ cup) risotto rice
60ml (4 tablespoons) sugar
1 vanilla pod
1 litre (4 cups) full cream milk (approximate amount)
125ml (½ cup) cream

fried pineapple
50g butter
1 small pineapple, peeled and sliced
60ml (4 tablespoons) citrus-based liqueur (Grand Marnier, Cointreau, Curaçao)

Tip the risotto rice and sugar into a medium, deep saucepan. Split the vanilla pod in half and add it to the rice with the milk. Bring to the boil and cook over medium heat, stirring occasionally at first and more frequently towards the end, until the rice grains are tender and the pudding is wonderfully thick. It should take about 25 minutes and the amount of milk required may vary, depending on the absorbency of the rice.

Remove from the heat, stir in the cream and discard the vanilla pod. (Now would be the time to add the vanilla extract or essence if you haven't used a pod.) Transfer the pudding to a bowl and cool, stirring occasionally to prevent a skin from forming.

fried pineapple Heat the butter in a large frying pan and fry the pineapple slices until golden brown on both sides. Add the liqueur and flame; the buttery pan-juices and booze will form the most delectable sauce.

to serve Spoon rice pudding onto plates (or into bowls) and doink fried pineapple on top. Finish the presentation with the sauce drizzled all about.

makeahead
You're welcome to serve this pudding warm or chilled, so it's fine to chill it for a day or two. The pineapple is best within an hour or so of being fried.

poshtip
Serve the rice pudding solo if you don't have the time, energy or enthusiasm to prepare the pineapple part of things.

poshquaffing
Much depends on whether or not the pudding flies solo or with its pineapple side-kick. Grand Marnier or Van der Hum, served chilled in your very best dessert wine glasses, or iced shot glasses, adds vivacity to the pud alone. Fried pineapple's added richness calls for a bit of effervescence. Semi-dry bubblies (carbonated or, better, in bottle fermented form) hit the honeyed spot with a lift.

vanilla pods, essence and extract are all very different. Posh chefs wouldn't be seen dead with anything but pods in their domain, and diligently split the bean and scrape out the seeds to flavour their creations. Vanilla pods are the fruit of a climbing orchid that flourishes in hot countries such as Mexico, where it originated, and Zanzibar, where I purchased bundles to bring home. Fresh pods are plump, glossy and brown; dried pods are shrivelled. Next best is vanilla extract, which is naturally flavoured. Vanilla essence is made from synthetic vanillin. Both, however, may be substituted if pods aren't at hand. As a substitute for one vanilla pod, use about 2ml (½ teaspoon) extract or 10ml (2 teaspoons) essence.

Rice pud throws off its homely label and tarts itself up in glam mode for this luxurious version, which will spoil you for all others. Fried pineapple flamed in liqueur adds a nice zing to things, counter-balancing the creaminess of the pudding.

chocolate chip
croissant pudding

The original version of bread and butter pud, a soul-soothing recipe dreamed up by the British, calls for sliced bread, liberally buttered and spread with apricot jam. This variation is way more luscious and calls for croissants instead of plain old bread. Make sure they're good, though, as inferior croissants will ruin the dish (and your reputation).

serves 8

1 litre (4 cups) full cream milk
1 vanilla pod, or 2ml (½ teaspoon) vanilla extract
5 eggs
200ml (¾ cup) castor sugar
300g croissants (about 6)
100g dark chocolate, chopped into chunks
whipped cream, to serve (optional)

Scald the milk in a medium saucepan. Remove from the heat. Split the vanilla pod in half and add to the milk. Whisk together the eggs and castor sugar until well blended. Gradually strain in the hot milk, stirring gently to avoid frothing. Stir in the vanilla extract if you aren't using a pod.

Slice the croissants thickly at a slant and arrange in a baking dish large enough to accommodate them in a single layer. Scatter chocolate chunks between the slices. Pour over the custard, and set aside for about 30 minutes to allow the custard to soak in.

Set the oven at 180ºC. Bake the pudding in a bain-marie for about 50 minutes until the custard has set and the croissants that peep out are crisp.

to serve Serve this heavenly dessert warm while the choc chips are still oozy, partnered (if you insist) with a spoonful of lightly whipped cream.

makeahead

This pud may be prepared several hours ahead, but is best baked about an hour before you sit down for dinner, leaving just enough time for it to cool slightly.

poshtip

When cooking with chocolate, only the best will do. Don't waste money on anything with less than 33% cocoa solids.

poshquaffing

This one's likely to set your feel-good serotonin levels soaring, so follow them with an amply cooled white muscadel, preferably young, fresh and fruity. Its late alcohol cuts the cream, unlike noble late harvests which, while valiant, tend to cloy this riot of flavour.

chocolate is one ingredient that you should never skimp on; the best comes from France, Belgium and Switzerland. Funny thing about a chocolate craving is that pigging out doesn't make it go away. Ask any chocaholic for whom life without a regular fix is simply not worth living and who cannot stop after munching a couple of blocks: that half-eaten slab keeps urging them back for more. There's no use discussing the matter with the good guys who stay on the culinary healthy, straight and narrow. They know nothing about it, and care even less.

chocolate volcanoes
with passion fruit sauce

The answer to any chocoholic's prayer. However, if cooked right through the charm is lost entirely, so follow the instructions carefully. Passion fruit sauce goes wonderfully on the side, but you could serve the volcanoes solo if you wish.

serves 8

passion fruit sauce
pulp of 6 granadillas (or 2 x 115g cans)
30ml (2 tablespoons) castor sugar
90ml (6 tablespoons) water
15ml (1 tablespoon) cornflour

200g dark chocolate, roughly chopped
200g unsalted butter, cut into blocks
30ml (2 tablespoons) rum or brandy
4 whole eggs
4 egg yolks
250ml (1 cup) sugar
125ml (½ cup) cake flour
icing sugar, for dusting

passion fruit sauce Mix the granadilla pulp and castor sugar in a small saucepan and bring to the boil. Mix the water and cornflour together, stir in, and simmer until the sauce thickens.

Heat the oven to 180°C. Grease eight metal dariole moulds and place on a baking tray. Melt the chocolate and butter in a bowl over simmering water. Remove from the heat and stir in the rum or brandy. Cool to room temperature.

Whisk together the eggs, egg yolks and sugar until thick and pale. Mix in the cooled chocolate. Sift in the flour and fold in. Pour the batter into the moulds and bake for 15 to 20 minutes; the surface should be crusty; the centres still runny (press gently with your finger to check).

to serve Turn the chocolate volcanoes out onto plates and pour passion fruit sauce around. To flossy up the presentation, sift icing sugar onto both volcanoes and plates.

makeahead

Chocolate volcanoes must be served promptly, but the batter can be mixed and the moulds filled an hour or two ahead. Passion fruit sauce may be refrigerated for up to three days.

poshquaffing

Risking certification as a wine bore, (very un-posh), this dessert evokes memories of a similarly rich repast enjoyed at Veuve Clicquot's Hotel du Marc where the House's Demi-Sec was served. A triumph! Local méthode cap classique versions' ambrosial bubbles lift the palate as majestically. Dry muscats, rare but worth seeking out, support with more restraint.

Chocolate heaven — puddings that ooze onto the plate when they've broken open.

irish coffee ice-cream
with whisky fudge sauce

This sinful dessert is hardly any trouble to make, just perfect when you want to show off but have no time to spare. You don't need an ice-cream machine, nor is there any call to rewhip the stuff while it freezes. To make things even simpler, you could forego the whisky fudge sauce for a dollop of whipped cream.

serves 8

100g brazil nuts
15ml (1 tablespoon) instant coffee granules
60ml (4 tablespoons) whisky
397g tin full-cream condensed milk
500ml (2 cups) cream

whisky fudge sauce
100g unsalted butter, cut into blocks
250ml (1 cup) brown sugar
45ml (3 tablespoons) cornflour
60ml (4 tablespoons) whisky
125ml (½ cup) cream

Chop the nuts fairly finely by hand or in a food processor, and roast in a dry frying pan over medium heat, tossing them about until they're nice and aromatic. Allow to cool.

Dissolve the coffee granules in the whisky in a large bowl. Mix in the condensed milk. Whip the cream stiffly, then fold in with three-quarters of the roasted nuts (reserve the rest for garnishing) until no streaks remain. Place in the freezer for about 2 hours until the ice-cream is half-frozen.

Stir the ice-cream gently, then spoon into a freezer-friendly container and freeze. It's fine to serve after about 4 hours, but will be firmer if frozen overnight.

whisky fudge sauce Combine the butter and brown sugar in medium saucepan. Stir over very low heat until the sugar dissolves. Mix the cornflour into the whisky, stir into the sauce and boil until it thickens. Remove from the heat and stir in the cream. Chill in the fridge.

to serve Pile neat ice-cream balls into bowls, drizzle over a little whisky fudge sauce, and top your creation with the reserved roasted nuts. Offer the remaining sauce in a jug in case your guests would like a little more.

makeahead

If you don't finish this ice-cream in one go (which is hardly likely), it may be kept in the freezer for up to three months. And, for easy serving, shape the ice-cream into balls and return to the freezer. Presentation is then quick-as-a-lick. Whisky fudge sauce may be refrigerated for a week.

poshtip

If you don't have any brazil nuts on hand, feel free to use almonds or hazelnuts instead.

poshquaffing

Iced coffee with a difference – shot with a tot or two of Ireland's finest whisky – dazzles alongside this confection. For vinous alternatives, look no further than the next wave of dessert wines: vin de paille. Straw wine (ripe grapes are dried, further concentrated on straw, even rooibos tea!) offers an unctuous texture with jasmine and quince interest.

Whisky and coffee are soulmates, most often teaming up in that heady hot drink that has rounded off dinner parties for longer than anyone can remember. The whisky does a great job of cutting the sweetness of the condensed milk in this ice-cream and the brown sugar in the sauce.

chocolate velvet ice-cream
with whipped cream

This exquisite, easy-to-make ice-cream poses a problem: who gets to lick the bowl/spoon/spatula? Be fair to everyone by making it in secret – while everyone's out of sight – and do the licking yourself!

serves 8 (fewer if they're chocoholics)

200ml (¾ cup) cocoa powder
250ml (1 cup) castor sugar
100g dark chocolate, roughly chopped
125ml (½ cup) strong black coffee
500ml (2 cups) cream
3 egg yolks
silver dragees, for garnishing

Sift the cocoa into a medium saucepan. Add the castor sugar, chocolate, coffee and 125ml (½ cup) of the cream. Stir over low heat until it comes to the boil and is well blended and smooth as velvet.

Beat the egg yolks until thick and pale (with an electric beater, or in a food processor). Add to the hot chocolate mixture and beat in well. Cool to room temperature.

Whip the remaining cream until thick enough to hold soft peaks. Set one-third aside in the fridge to serve with the ice-cream, and fold the rest into the chocolate mixture. Spoon into individual serving bowls or glasses (or coffee cups) and freeze until firm.

to serve Spoon a little of the reserved whipped cream onto each serving as it comes from the freezer. Garnish generously with silver dragees to add sparkle to the proceedings.

makeahead
Hard as it is to imagine (this ice-cream is normally polished off in one go), it will be fine in the freezer for up to two months.

poshtip
To add nuttiness, roughly crumble 100g walnuts, roast in a frying pan until golden and aromatic, and fold in with the cream.

poshquaffing
A trusty option for both chocolate and real ice-cream (difficult wine partners) is good, dry, bottle-fermented sparkling wine. No need to overshoot with vintage or prestige cuvée labels, as entry-level brut's mousse puts the cream into relief just fine. On cooler nights, a noble late harvest offers home-hearth succour.

cocoa is an ancient drink, dreamed up by the Aztecs and introduced to the rest of the world via Spanish conquerors. Cocoa beans, about the size of almonds, grow in large pods on a tree found in Africa and tropical America. En route to becoming the powder we all know and love, the beans are fermented and roasted, then shelled and ground. Dense chocolate liquid is extracted, which contains cocoa butter, the core ingredient of coffee.

wicked bitter chocolate loaf
with wild cherries

makes 1 small loaf; serves 8 to 10

60ml (¼ cup) cognac or brandy
125ml (½ cup) bleached sultanas
200g dark chocolate, roughly chopped
125g soft unsalted butter, cut into blocks
2ml (½ teaspoon) vanilla extract
60ml (4 tablespoons) cocoa powder
100g ground almonds
125ml (½ cup) cake flour
pinch salt
3 eggs, separated
200ml (¾ cup) castor sugar
100g cherries, for garnishing (optional)

chocolate glaze
60ml (4 tablespoons) cream
200g dark chocolate, roughly chopped
30g (2 tablespoons) unsalted butter

Heat the oven to 170ºC. Line a small (23cm) loaf tin with non-stick baking paper. Pour the cognac or brandy over the sultanas in a bowl and set aside to plump up.

Melt the chocolate and butter in a large bowl set in a pan of simmering water. Stir in the vanilla extract, sultanas and brandy. Sift in the cocoa, and fold in. Cool to room temperature.

Add the almonds, flour and salt, and fold in. Beat the egg yolks and castor sugar in a food processor or with an electric mixer until thick and pale. Stir in. Beat the egg whites to soft peaks and fold in.

Pour the batter into the prepared loaf tin and bake for 50 to 60 minutes until a skewer comes out clean. Cool the cake in the tin for about 10 minutes, then turn out onto a rack and cool.

chocolate glaze Heat the cream in a small saucepan to boiling point. Remove from the heat, add the chocolate and allow it to soften. Add the butter and beat until smooth.

to serve Place the loaf on a plate and spread with chocolate glaze while it's still warm. Arrange cherries on top. Allow the glaze to set before slicing the cake with a hot, wet serrated knife.

This little loaf packs a hefty punch; a sliver will satisfy the most ardent chocolate lover. The decadent glaze isn't strictly necessary, but it does make the loaf look more elegant And, for economic reasons, cheap brandy will happily pose for cognac.

the ultimate
lemon tart

It's hard to imagine life without lemons. Their fragrant tang adds a zap to everything from vinaigrette to just-shucked oysters. Here their soaring flavour is the hero of a classy tart. You could also make individual tarts if you wish; the recipe will make six.

serves 8

shortcrust pastry
250ml (1 cup) cake flour
pinch salt
45ml (3 tablespoons) castor sugar
50g butter, cut into small cubes
finely grated zest of 1 lemon
1 egg yolk
30ml (2 tablespoons) iced water

lemon filling
3 eggs, lightly beaten
200ml (¾ cup) castor sugar
finely grated zest and juice of 4 lemons
250ml (1 cup) cream
icing sugar, for dusting

shortcrust pastry To make by hand: sift the flour, salt and castor sugar into a bowl. Add the butter and lemon zest and rub in until the mixture is crumbly. Make a well in the mixture, add the egg yolk and water, and knead with your fingers to a smooth dough.

To prepare the pastry in a food processor: sift the flour and castor sugar into the bowl. Add the butter and lemon zest and whiz until finely crumbled. Add the egg yolk and water, and whiz until the dough forms a ball. Wrap in clingfilm and refrigerate for 30 minutes to rest.

Set the oven at 180°C. Grease a 26cm loose-based flan tin. Roll out the pastry on a lightly floured surface and neatly line the flan tin. Bake for 15 to 20 minutes until the pastry is crisp and very lightly coloured. Reduce the oven heat to 160°C.

lemon filling Whisk together the eggs, castor sugar and lemon zest until thick and foamy. Stir in the lemon juice. Whip the cream to soft peaks and fold in. Pour the cold filling into the hot pastry (so the pastry seals and hold the filling) and bake for about 30 minutes until set.

to serve Heat the oven grill. As the tart emerges from the oven, sift icing sugar on top and grill briefly to caramelize the sugar.

makeahead

The uncooked pastry shell may be refrigerated for up to a day before being baked. The baked tart needs to be served cool and can be chilled in the fridge for a day. Caramelize the icing sugar shortly before serving.

poshtip

To extract the most juice as possible from lemons, prick the skin all over and microwave on full power for 10 to 15 seconds. Cut in half and squeeze, baby, squeeze. When grating the rind, avoid the bitter white pith like the plague.

poshquaffing

Noble late harvest wines gain their character from botrytis cinerea. Not all are uniform though, as the original grape adds its pound of flesh. Weisser (real) riesling imparts a delectable mineral tang, a perfect foil here. For something less exuberant, a simple bubbly made from sauvignon blanc spars with the citrus and elevates the cream.

farmhouse-style
warm fruit pie

There's something wonderfully comforting about a fruit pie served warm from the oven.
Not to mention the blissful smell as it bakes, filling the house with happiness.

serves 8 to 10

shortcrust pastry (page 178)
2 x 425g tins stoned cherries
125g soft butter
160ml (1¼ cups) castor sugar
2 eggs, lightly beaten
100g crushed almonds
45ml (3 tablespoons) cake flour
1ml (¼ teaspoon) almond essence
30ml (2 tablespoons) sugar
icing sugar, for dusting

Roll out the pastry and line a 24cm tart pan. Chill it the fridge while preparing the filling. Set the oven at 200°C.

Drain the cherries well, blotting the excess moisture with paper towels. Pour the syrup into a small saucepan and boil uncovered until reduced and thickened to a light glaze. Pour into a jug and chill in the fridge.

Beat together the butter and castor sugar until pale and fluffy. Beat in the eggs. Add the almonds, flour and almond essence, and mix in well.

Spread the almond mixture into the unbaked pastry shell. Arrange the cherries on top and sprinkle with sugar. Bake for 15 minutes, then reduce the oven temperature to 160°C and bake for about 45 minutes more until set. Cool the pie in the tin.

to serve Dust the pie generously with icing sugar, and serve warm. It's delish as is, or you could go the whole hog and add whipped cream or vanilla ice-cream.

makeahead

This pie is best on the day it's made, but you don't have to be too fussy about it. Just don't chill it as the flavour won't be as pronounced.

poshtip

When plums are in season, use them instead of cherries. You'll need 7 or 8. Cut around the circumferance to the pips, twist the halves apart and discard the pips. Place cut-side down on kitchen paper to drain while preparing the pastry.

poshquaffing

Evocative of winter hearths, this pie calls for warming wine fare. Sweet reds, edging back into fashion, are just the ticket. Examples from pinotage, ruby cabernet, even merlot, offer ripe fruit without stealing the plum's show. Seek out natural grape-sweet versions as fortifying alcohol gets in the way. Berries? Well, they zest with lively pink bubbly.

Sifted icing sugar flossies up the plainest pie, even when it's presented in the tin.

pear pastries
with goat's cheese and gorgonzola

Cheese and fruit are great mates. Pile them onto puff pastry and, as they bake, they merge luxuriously together for a memorable sweet-savoury finish to a meal with layers of flavours. If fresh figs are in season, slice them and mix with the pears.

serves 6

400g puff pastry
1 egg
15ml (1 tablespoon) milk
2 pears
freshly squeezed juice of 1 lemon
100g goat's cheese
50g gorgonzola or blue cheese

Heat the oven to 200ºC. Defrost the pastry, unroll it and cut into 6 squares. Place on a lightly oiled baking sheet. Whisk together the egg and milk and brush a little around the edges of the pastry (offer the rest to the cat).

Peel, halve, core and thinly slice the pears into a bowl. Pour over the lemon juice and toss to coat well. Slice the goat's cheese. Pile the pears and goat's cheese onto the pastries and crumble gorgonzola or blue cheese on top.

Bake for 15 to 20 minutes until the pastries are crisp and golden and the cheese has melted. Turn on the oven grill for a few minutes if necessary, for extra colour.

to serve Serve these tarts warm, preferably not too long after they've been baked. The cheese will toughen as it cools, which is not at all appealing.

gorgonzola, Italy's famous blue-veined cheese, was once exclusive to the village of that name, but is now produced all over the world. Often described as an early copy of France's renowned roquefort cheese, it's milder, softer, creamier and less salty. Perfectly ripe gorgonzola is springy to the touch and has a slightly musty smell. It should have very little rind, and should be smooth and cream-coloured, marbled with blue-grey or blue-green.

The end!